LOVE & LIGHT

DISPLAYING

GODLY CHARACTER

Roshan Seneviratne

Trafford
PUBLISHING™

Order this book online at www.trafford.com
or email orders@trafford.com

Most Trafford titles are also available at major online book retailers.

Note for Librarians: A cataloguing record for this book is available from Library
and Archives Canada at www.collectionscanada.ca/amicus/index-e.html

Printed in Victoria, BC, Canada.

ISBN: 978-1-4251-6026-5

*Our mission is to efficiently provide the world's finest, most comprehensive
book publishing service, enabling every author to experience success.
To find out how to publish your book, your way, and have it available
worldwide, visit us online at www.trafford.com*

Trafford rev. 9/24/2009

www.trafford.com

North America & international
toll-free: 1 888 232 4444 (USA & Canada)
phone: 250 383 6864 ♦ fax: 812 355 4082

Dedication

To God, for this book

To Emily, my wife, for her unending love and support

To Sarah and Daniel, my precious children,
who allowed me the time to write this

To Verity, for all her help and assistance,
and magnificent cover design

To Susan and Vandana, for their faith and generosity

To my parents who always believed in me

To John F. MacArthur, for his inspirational
commentary on 1 Corinthians

Preface

This book is the first *Keys For Life* to be published. It's primary function is to help Christians with their walk with God.

It is written in a simple, concise manner, for both personal study and reflection, and may also be used to teach from. In fact, the content is such that, you may begin teaching from the very first line.

This particular topic deals with two of the most prominent characteristics of God: Love and Light.

It is what we, as Christians, are to display in our lives, and it is meant to be what separates us from all other religions. Jesus said that we are the light of the world, and commanded us to love one another. Accordingly, He expects both from us. And, in fact, we are going to be judged on both accounts.

Therefore, it is essential that we receive the proper insight and instruction, if we are to fulfil the calling God placed on our life in this regard, and be all that God designed, and destined us to be.

If you are truly serious about following Christ's example, and displaying His character in your life, then this book is a must for you. It is not a simple journey, but an extremely rewarding one.

The *Keys For Life* series contain essential truth for everyday Christian living. It is my hope that you keep them close to you, and not just come to know the material but do it. In the words of the apostle James, in James chapter 1, verses 22 and 25: *"Do not merely listen to (or in this case read) the word, and so deceive yourselves. Do what it says... and if you do what it says and don't forget what you've heard (or read), then* **God will bless you for doing it.**"

Table of Contents

Chapter 1 God Is Light   5
❧ The Essence Of God's Nature & Character   5
❧ GOD IS LIGHT   7
❧ GOD HAS NO DARKNESS IN HIM AT ALL   8
❧ YOU ARE LIGHT   10
  ❤ First Fruit Of Light: Goodness   11
  ❤ Second Fruit Of Light: Righteousness   13
  ❤ Third Fruit Of Light: Truth   17
❧ LOVE & LIGHT – WORKING TOGETHER   18

Chapter 2 The Commandment To Love   21
❧ GOD IS LOVE   21
  ❤ A New Commandment   22
  ❤ The Royal Law   24
  ❤ A More Excellent Way   25
❧ A LOOK AT THE GOD-KIND OF LOVE   26
  ❤ A Love Of The Heart, Soul & Mind   28
  ❤ The Primary Motivation   29
  ❤ An Overview Of What Love Is & What Love Does   31

Chapter 3 Love's Patience & Forgiveness   32
❧ LOVE SUFFERS LONG   32
  ❤ The Importance Of Operating In Patient Love   33
❧ LOVE'S FORGIVENESS   35
  ❤ Forgiveness & Conflict Resolution   37
❧ PATIENCE & FORGIVENESS – TWO INSEPARABLE QUALITIES   39
  ❤ Being Willing To Forgive   43

Chapter 4 Love's Kindness   45
❧ EXPRESSIONS OF KINDNESS   45
  ❤ The Law Of Kindness – Governing What You Say   47
  ❤ Kindness As Active Good Will   49
  ❤ How Will You Be Remembered?   53

Chapter 5 Love – Not Envious Or Jealous 56
    ❧ Love Does Not Envy 56
      ❤ *Jealousy That Covets What Is Others* 58
      ❤ *Jealousy That Desires Evil For Others* 59

Chapter 6 Love Does Not Brag Or Boast 62
    ❧ Boasting & Bragging – The Other Side Of Jealousy 62
      ❤ *The Church At Corinth* 63
      ❤ *Jesus Christ – Our Example* 64

Chapter 7 Love – Not Proud Or Arrogant 67
    ❧ Pride & Arrogance 67
      ❤ *The Sin God Hates* 68
      ❤ *Different Forms Of Pride* 69
      ❤ *Pride's Opposite: Humility* 71
      ❤ *Humble Yourself Before God* 73
      ❤ *Blessed Are The Meek* 74

Chapter 8 Love Is Not Rude 78
    ❧ Behaviour Contrary To Love 78
      ❤ *Godly Behaviour* 80

Chapter 9 Love – Not Selfish Or Self-Centred 82
    ❧ Love Does Not Seek It's Own 82
      ❤ *Putting Others First* 83
      ❤ *Forget About Yourself* 84

Chapter 10 Love Is Not Provoked Easily 87
    ❧ Love – Not Irritated, Upset Or Angry 87
      ❤ *Righteous Anger* 87
      ❤ *Unrighteous Anger* 89
      ❤ *Wisdom To Control Your Anger* 90

Chapter 11 Love Does Not Rejoice In Iniquity 92
    ❧ Love Does No Wrong 92
      ❤ *Rejoicing Over Another's Downfall* 93
      ❤ *Hurting People With The Truth* 94

Chapter 12 Love Rejoices In The Truth   96
   ✤ Love's Two-Fold 'Truth'   96
     ♥ *Factual Truth*   96
     ♥ *God's Word As Truth*   98
     ♥ *Speaking The Truth In Love*   99

Chapter 13 Love Bears All Things   101
   ✤ Love's Protective Nature   101
     ♥ *Love's Ability To Put Up With Anything*   103

Chapter 14 Love Believes All Things   105
   ✤ Love's Eagerness To Believe The Best   105
     ♥ *It's The Thought That Counts*   106
   ✤ Love's Opposite – Believing The Worst   107

Chapter 15 Love Hopes All Things   109
   ✤ Love's Hope   109

Chapter 16 Love Endures All Things   112
   ✤ Love's Tenacity & Perseverance   112
     ♥ *Never Failing Love*   113

Chapter 17 The Benefits & Manifestations Of Love   115
   ✤ A Look At Galatians 5:22-23   115
     ♥ *Love's Joy – Inner Strength*   116
     ♥ *Love's Peace – Inward Stability*   117
   ✤ Never Ending Light & Never Failing Love   119

Chapter 1

GOD IS LIGHT

✤ The Essence Of God's Nature & Character

Ephesians chapter 5, verses 1 and 2 tell us to "**Be imitators of God**, therefore, as dearly loved children and **live a life of love**, just as Christ loved us and gave himself up for us as a fragrant offering and sacrifice to God."[NIV]

This is easier said that done. To imitate God, we must first know what God is like. And it cannot be just what others have said, or opinions we've formed through our own experiences, but what the Bible actually says about Him.

The Bible has a great deal to say about God. But of all the things it does say about Him, such as Him being *faithful, true, trustworthy*[1], *gracious, merciful*[2], *holy*[3], *a consuming fire*[4], *a sun and shield*[5], and

---

[1]   **2 Cor 1:18** But as God is true (Gk. 'sure, trustworthy, faithful'), our word toward you was not yea and nay. [KJV]

[2]   **Psa 116:5** Gracious is the LORD, and righteous; yea, our God is merciful. [KJV]; **2 Chr 30:9b** ... the LORD your God is gracious and merciful, and will not turn away his face from you, if ye return unto him. [KJV]

[3]   **Psa 99:9** Exalt the LORD our God, and worship at his holy hill; for the LORD our God is holy. [KJV]

[4]   **Heb 12:29** For our God is a consuming fire. [KJV]

[5]   **Psa 84:11** For the LORD God is a sun and shield: the LORD will give grace and glory: no good thing will he withhold from them that walk uprightly. [KJV]

so on, there are two particular qualities that seem to stand above all others, and not only *describe* all that He is, but also *explains* all that He does: They are *Love* and *Light*.

The *First* is found in 1ˢᵗ *John chapter 4, verses 8 and 16* which tell us that 'GOD IS LOVE'[6], with verse 16 going on to elaborate…

1 John 4:16 *And we have known and believed the love that God hath to us. GOD IS LOVE; and he that dwelleth in love dwelleth in God, and God in him.* KJV

The *Second* is found in 1ˢᵗ John chapter 1 and verse 5, where the apostle John writes…

1 John 1:5 *This then is the message which we have heard of him (Jesus), and declare unto you, that GOD IS LIGHT, and in Him is no darkness at all.* KJV

Contained within these statements is the very *essence* of Who, and What God is.

What's more, it also shows us that *love* and *light* operate in perfect harmony with each other, even though one *exposes sin*[7] while the other *covers it*[8]. And if God can do it, then so must we.

Also, since *God is light* and *God is love*, and everything in this universe, according to Colossians 1:16, were 'made by Him and for Him', then everything has its origin in both love and light, and has been pre-programmed to respond to it.

Therefore, if either is missing in a persons life, there will always be something lacking, unfulfilled, or just wrong with their life, whether it's immediately noticeable or not.

---

6   **1 John 4:8** *He that loveth not knoweth not God; for God is love.* KJV

7   **Eph 5:11** *Have nothing to do with the fruitless deeds of darkness, but rather expose them.* NIV

8   **Prov 10:12** *Hatred stirs up strife, But love covers all sins.* NKJV & **1 Pet 4:8** *And above all things have fervent love for one another, for "love will cover a multitude of sins."* NKJV

❧ GOD IS LIGHT

Let's begin by looking at, and identifying, *what light is*, and *what light does.*

Returning to 1st John chapter 1 and verse 5, the apostle John again writes...

1 John 1:5 *This then is the message which we have heard of him (Jesus), and declare unto you, that GOD IS LIGHT, and in Him is NO DARKNESS AT ALL.* KJV

Science now tells us that light is the source of all life. In other words, everything in existence today, has its origins in light, a fact that the Bible has maintained from the very beginning when it said, *"In the beginning God (Who is light) created the heavens and the earth"* (**Genesis 1:1 &** 1st **John 1:5**).

Technically speaking, what we perceive as 'light' today, is actually a very small portion of the *electromagnetic spectrum.* The entire range includes: *Gamma rays, hard and soft X-rays, Ultraviolet radiation,* **Visible light,** *Infrared radiation, Microwaves, and Radio waves*[9] (in that order).

And from science we know that, not only does *Visible light* illuminate and reveals what's in the dark, but *X-rays* penetrate and reveal what's on the inside, *Infrared* let's us actually see in the dark (when something doesn't want to reveal itself), and as we all know, *Radio waves* speak to us,

From a theological perspective, we get a better understanding of how God being light not only constantly *communicates* with us, but also looks *at us,* and *right through us.* That's why the Bible says in 1st Corinthians chapter 4, and the latter half of verse 5...

1 Cor 4:5b *He (God) will bring to light what is hidden in darkness and will expose the motives of men's hearts.* NIV

---

9   "Electromagnetic Radiation," Microsoft(R) Encarta(R) 98 Encyclopedia. (c) 1993-1997 Microsoft Corporation. All rights reserved.

In addition to this *electromagnetic spectrum* is also the *electromagnetic field*. It is this field that not only surrounds the earth, but allows life to exist here.

Without this electromagnetic field, the cells in your body would not be able to communicate with themselves, or any of the surrounding cells.

And without cell communication, your eyes wouldn't even be able understand what it was looking at, let alone communicate to your brain, so that it could tell your body what to do about it.

This gives even further insight into *Acts 17:28* that declares, *"For in him we live and move and have our being."*

❧ GOD HAS NO DARKNESS IN HIM AT ALL

Only *light* is capable of all this, *not* darkness.

Therefore, it makes perfect sense that the apostle John wouldn't just stop at saying 'God *is light*', but would go on to *insist* that 'in Him *is no darkness at all*'.

However, in spite of everything we've just looked at, people still insist that, from a spiritual perspective, there is a 'dark side' to God that punishes His people and does them harm 'to teach them a lesson'. But what they often forget is that, not only is God *light*, but *love* as well.

The apostle James understood how people think and made it clear in his writings, in James chapter 1 and verse 17 that...

James 1:17 EVERY good gift and EVERY perfect gift is from above, and comes down from the Father of lights, with whom there is no variation or shadow of turning. NKJV

Notice here that 'every good and every perfect gift' is attributed to *light*, not *love*, showing us that they both *can*, and *do* work together in perfect harmony, *giving us the very best*, with *no regrets*.

Even in the case of discipline, the Scriptures teach us that, God only *judges* those outside His family according to Romans chapter 12 and verse 19, which says…

Rom 12:19 *Beloved, never avenge yourselves, but leave room for the wrath of God; for it is written, "Vengeance is mine, I will repay, says the Lord."* NRSV

And when it comes to those who *belong to God's family*, Hebrews chapter 12 and verse 6 says…

Heb 12:6 *For whom the Lord loveth He chasteneth, and scourgeth every son whom He receiveth.* KJV

In other words, if you have been wronged by someone outside God's Family, *Romans 12* says that God Himself *will* avenge you.

However, if you've been wronged by a Christian brother or sister, then *Hebrews 12* says that *God* will discipline them *His* way; Please note that THE LORD does this, NOT you.[10]

As for those of us who think they have been called to correct others, I have a verse for you; It is found in Hebrews chapter 13 and verse 1, where the writer of Hebrews says…

Heb 13:1 *Continue to LOVE each other with true Christian love.* NLT

As to how we are to love one another, and the world around us, that's what we will be covering in this book in some detail.

And as to the question of how all this *relates to us*, not only does John say that 'God is light' in 1ˢᵗ John 1:5 (which refers to both *light*[11] and *glory*[12] in Scripture), but in John chapter 8 and verse 12 it says…

---

10   All this will be covered in some detail in the series on *'Judgement and Destruction'.*

11   **Rev 22:5** *There shall be no night there: They need no lamp nor light of the sun, for the Lord God gives them light. And they shall reign forever and ever.* NKJV

12   **Ezek 10:4b** *… and the court was full of the brightness of the Lord's glory.* NKJV

John 8:12 *Then spake Jesus again unto them, saying, I am the light of the world: he that followeth me shall not walk in darkness, but shall have the light of life.* KJV

And just so we don't think He meant it in a spiritual sense only, in Matthew chapter 17, verses 1 through 3 it says…

Mat 17:1 *And after six days Jesus taketh Peter, James, and John his brother, and bringeth them up into an high mountain apart,*

Mat 17:2 *And was transfigured before them: and his face did shine as the sun, and his raiment was white as the light.*

Mat 17:3 *And, behold, there appeared unto them Moses and Elias talking with him.* KJV

So, when Jesus talked about being '*the light of the world*', He actually meant it in both a *literal* and *spiritual* sense.

❧ You Are Light

Not only is Jesus 'the light of the world', but in Matthew chapter 5 and verse 14, Jesus said of *us*…

Mat 5:14 *You are the light of the world. A city that is set on a hill cannot be hidden.* NKJV

In relation to what we've already seen about our origins and light, this verse takes on new meaning, especially when we consider what happened to Moses in Exodus chapter 34 and verse 29, where it says…

Exo 34:29b *As he came down from the mountain with the two tablets of the covenant in his hand, Moses did not know that the skin of his face shone because he had been talking with God.* NRSV

Now, regardless of whether or not we as believers will eventually walk in this kind of light, we are still commanded to *walk in the light* in a *spiritual sense*, throughout the Bible.

In Paul's first encounter with Jesus on the road to Damascus in Acts chapter 26, among other things, he was given the commission in verse 18…

Acts 26:18 To open their eyes, and to turn them from darkness to light, and from the power of Satan unto God, that they may receive forgiveness of sins (not exposed and harmed), and inheritance among them which are sanctified by faith that is in me. KJV

In fact, Peter confirms this when He says in 1ˢᵗ Peter chapter 2 and verse 9…

1 Pet 2:9 But you are a chosen generation, a royal priesthood, a holy nation, His own special people, that you may proclaim the praises of Him who called you out of darkness into His marvellous light; NKJV

In other words, this is part of our 'calling' and *destiny*: To walk in 'His *marvellous light'*.

♥ *First Fruit Of Light: Goodness*

In order to get some insight into what this actually means, we must turn to Ephesians chapter 5, and look at verse 8 through 10 where the apostle Paul reveals what *walking in the light* involves as he writes…

Eph 5:8 For you were once darkness, but now YOU ARE LIGHT in the Lord. LIVE as CHILDREN OF LIGHT

Eph 5:9 (for the fruit of the LIGHT consists in all GOODNESS, RIGHTEOUSNESS and TRUTH)

Eph 5:10 and ('examine, put to the test[13] *and…) find out what pleases the Lord.* NIV

In other words, when we look at light *spiritually*, it consists of *'goodness, righteousness and truth'* (none of which can be achieved in the flesh).

Now, except for the King James, and New King James Versions, all others translate this verse correctly as *'the fruit of light'*; It is not *'the fruit of the spirit'*; The fruit of the spirit is found in Galatians chapter 5 and verses 22 and 23.

As to *the fruit of LIGHT* (as described here), it again, has *three spiritual characteristics* or *'works'*, that God expects *all of us* to walk in (as *'children of light'* [vs.8]), with the first being *'GOODNESS'*.

William Hendriksen describes *'goodness'* as being *"spirit created, moral, and spiritual excellence of every description"*[14]; R. Kent Hughes says it's *'generosity'*[15]; And John MacArthur adds that it has its *'fullest and highest expression in that which is willingly and sacrificially done for others.'*[16]

In 2nd Thessalonians 1:11, the apostle Paul encourages the Thessalonians by saying…

2 Th 1:11 To this end also we pray for you always that our God may count you worthy of your calling, and fulfil every desire for goodness and the work of faith with power; NASB

---

13   Peter T. O'Brien, *The Letter To The Ephesians*, copyright © 1999 Wm. B. Eerdmans Publishing Company, 255 Jefferson Ave. S.E., Grand Rapids, Michigan 49503. and in the U.K. by APOLLOS, 38 De Montfort Street, Leicester, England LE1 7GP p.369

14   William Hendriksen, *'Galatians, Ephesians, Philippians, Colossians, and Philemon'*, Baker Books, Grand Rapids, Michigan. 49516. July 2002 *Ephesians* p.231-232

15   R. Kent Hughes, *Ephesians*, Copyright © 1990 by R. Kent Hughes, Published by Crossways Books, A division of Good News Publishers, 1300 Crescent Street, Wheaton, Illinois. 60187. p.165

16   John F. MacArthur, *The MacArthur New Testament Commentary*, *Ephesians*, copyright © 1986 by The Moody Bible Institute of Chicago, p.209

♥ *Second Fruit Of Light: Righteousness*

The second characteristic of light is 'RIGHTEOUSNESS'.

Hendriksen says that 'RIGHTEOUSNESS' is "*the joy of doing what is right in the eyes of God, walking the straight path and never deviating from it*"[17]; R. Kent Hughes refers to it as '*integrity in all dealings with God and man*'[18].

In relation to '*doing what is right in the eyes of God*', the apostle Paul writes in Romans chapter 4, verses 1 through 8...

Rom 4:1 What then shall we say that Abraham our father has found according to the flesh?

Rom 4:2 For if Abraham was justified by works, he has something to boast about, but not before God.

Rom 4:3 For what does the Scripture say? "Abraham believed God, and it was accounted to him for righteousness."

Rom 4:4 Now to him who works, the wages are not counted as grace but as debt.

Rom 4:5 But to him who does not work but believes on Him who justifies the ungodly, his faith is accounted for righteousness,

Rom 4:6 just as David also describes the blessedness of the man to whom God imputes righteousness apart from works:

Rom 4:7 "Blessed are those whose lawless deeds are forgiven, And whose sins are covered;

---

17   William Hendriksen, '*Galatians, Ephesians, Philippians, Colossians, and Philemon*', Baker Books, Grand Rapids, Michigan. 49516. July 2002 *Ephesians* p.231-232

18   R. Kent Hughes, *Ephesians*, Copyright © 1990 by R. Kent Hughes, Published by Crossways Books, A division of Good News Publishers, 1300 Crescent Street, Wheaton, Illinois. 60187. p.165

Rom 4:8 Blessed is the man to whom the LORD shall not impute sin." NKJV

In other words, faith is an integral part of our right-standing with God; In fact, the above Scripture shows us that, Old Testament and New, righteousness has always been by faith, not works.

Added to this Scripture in Romans chapter 4, Paul goes even further in Ephesians chapter 4, verses 22 through 24 and says...

Eph 4:22 You were taught to put away your former way of life, your old self, corrupt and deluded by its lusts,

Eph 4:23 and to be renewed in the spirit of your minds,

Eph 4:24 and to clothe yourselves with the new self, created according to the likeness of God in true righteousness and holiness. NRSV

Although Ephesians 5:9 doesn't mention it, *righteousness* and *holiness* are very closely related.

In fact, one of light's defining attributes is *holiness,* defined as *'moral perfection, freedom from blemish of any kind, separate from others and unique'* just like God is; Exodus chapter 15, verses 11 through 13 says...

Exo 15:11 Who is like You, O LORD, among the gods? Who is like You, glorious in holiness (notice the close tie between 'glory' and 'holiness'), Fearful in praises, doing wonders?

Exo 15:12 You stretched out Your right hand; The earth swallowed them.

Exo 15:13 You in Your mercy have led forth The people whom You have redeemed; You have guided them in Your strength To Your holy habitation. NKJV

Notice that God's *glory* and *holiness* is not without *mercy*; That is *extremely significant*.

So many people today operate in what they believe is *holiness*, but it is without *mercy*, which immediately precludes it from being *'holy'*, since it is no longer *'morally perfect'*, and therefore, *harmful* and *dangerous*.

It's *harmful* because it *scrutinizes*, *exposes* and *humiliates* people, leaving them *downcast*, *disheartened* and *defeated*, which is exactly what the devil wants. Therefore, if he can orchestrate the sin, and get you to expose it *'in the name of God'*, then he has won.

And what's worse is that he will make you think that you are doing God's work, when all the time, you're working for him, and behaving just the way he does according to Revelation chapter 12 and verse 10 which said…

Rev 12:10 *Then I heard a loud voice saying in heaven, "Now salvation, and strength, and the kingdom of our God, and the power of His Christ have come, for the accuser of our brethren, who accused them before our God day and night, has been cast down.* NKJV

And that's what satan does; *Expose* and *accuse* the brethren day and night, showing no *mercy* (God's undeserved *love*) or *grace* (God's undeserved *favour*) toward them, since he is God's total opposite in all things.

Now, added to being harmful, the reason it is *dangerous* to be *'holy'* without being *merciful* is because you set yourself up as *'judge'* over others, to which Jesus says in Luke chapter 6 and verse 37…

Luke 6:37 *Judge not, and you shall not be judged. Condemn not, and you shall not be condemned. Forgive, and you will be forgiven.* NKJV

Further to this, in Matthew chapter 7, verses 1 through 5, Jesus also adds…

Mat 7:1 *Stop judging others, and you will not be judged.*

Mat 7:2 For others will treat you as you treat them. Whatever measure you use in judging others, it will be used to measure how you are judged.

Mat 7:3 Why worry about a speck in your friend's eye when you have a log (this is 'the log' of judging others) in your own?

Mat 7:4 How can you think of saying, 'Friend, let me help you get rid of that speck in your eye,' when you can't see past the log in your own eye?

Mat 7:5 Hypocrite! First get rid of the log (of judgement) from your own eye; then perhaps you will see well enough to deal with the speck (of sin – great or small) in your friend's eye. NLT mod.

True holiness and righteousness is full of *love, grace* and *mercy.*

Without it you are no different to satan himself, who can appear as *an angel of light* and use that light to destroy people with according to 2ⁿᵈ Corinthians chapter 11, verses 13 through 15, where the apostle Paul writes…

2 Cor 11:13 For such are false apostles, deceitful workers, transforming themselves into apostles of Christ.

2 Cor 11:14 And no wonder! For Satan himself transforms himself into an angel of light.

2 Cor 11:15 Therefore it is no great thing if his ministers also transform themselves into ministers of righteousness, whose end will be according to their works. NKJV

In other words, if what they do as *'apostles of Christ'* ends up causing grief and heartache, even though they insist that they are *'ministers of righteousness'*, Paul says that their *'end'* proves that they are, in fact, *'false apostles'*, and satan's own *ministers.*

There is a difference between being a *'child'*, and being a *'judge'*, when it come to *light*: We were never made '*judges in light*', but are '*children of light*', meaning that we were to *let our light shine* and *bless others* with it; Never *harm* and *expose* them.

That's why Ephesians 5:10 (following vs.9's '*the fruit of light*') goes on to say, "('*examine, put to the test*'[19] and) *find out what pleases the Lord*"; Because what *you think* pleases the Lord, and what *actually* pleases Him, may be two entirely different things.

This applies to both ministry, and your general, daily activities (which includes *social, family, work* and so on).

Before we move on to the last *fruit of light*, if you're interested in as to *why* the apostle Paul listed '*goodness*' ahead of '*righteousness*', the answer is found in what he says in Romans chapter 5 and verse 7, and that is…

Rom 5:7 Indeed, rarely will anyone die for a righteous person--though perhaps for a good person someone might actually dare to die. [NRSV]

There's a lesson in this: It is better to develop '*goodness*' ahead of '*righteousness*' if you want to avoid being *proud, self-righteous* and *self-centred.*

♥ *Third Fruit Of Light: Truth*

This brings us to the third, and final *characteristic of light*, as mentioned in Ephesians 5:9, and that is '*TRUTH*'.

MacArthur says it best, when he writes, "*TRUTH has to do with honesty, reliability, trustworthiness, and integrity – in contrast to the hypocritical, deceptive, and false ways of the old life of darkness.*"[20]

19　Peter T. O'Brien, *The Letter To The Ephesians,* copyright © 1999 Wm. B. Eerdmans Publishing Company, 255 Jefferson Ave. S.E., Grand Rapids, Michigan 49503. and in the U.K. by APOLLOS, 38 De Montfort Street, Leicester, England LE1 7GP p.369

20　John F. MacArthur, *The MacArthur New Testament Commentary, Ephesians,* copyright © 1986 by The Moody Bible Institute of Chicago, p.210

As *children of light* we are to bear resemblance to the Heavenly Father Who *'is light'*, and produce *the fruit of light* in our lives.

And since God is both *light* and *love*, all these *fruits of light* that we are to walk in must come from a *heart of love* as described in 1st Corinthians 13 which we will look at in some detail right after this.

❧ LOVE & LIGHT – WORKING TOGETHER

As to how *light*, which *exposes* true evil, and *love*, which *covers* a multitude of sins, are to work together in harmony is best seen in what Jesus did in John chapter 8, verses 2 through 12, where it says…

John 8:2 Now early in the morning He came again into the temple, and all the people came to Him; and He sat down and taught them.

John 8:3 Then the scribes and Pharisees brought to Him a woman caught in adultery. And when they had set her in the midst,

John 8:4 they said to Him, "Teacher, this woman was caught in adultery, in the very act.

John 8:5 "Now Moses, in the law, commanded us that such should be stoned. But what do You say?"

John 8:6 This they said, testing Him, that they might have something of which to accuse Him. But Jesus stooped down and wrote on the ground with His finger, as though He did not hear. NKJV

Notice the kind of spirit that wanted to *'bring to the light'* and *expose* this woman's sin to the world: It was a *religious, demonic, Pharisaical* spirit; Just like those Paul talked about in 2nd

Corinthians 11, verses 13 through 15.[21] Following this, verse 7 goes on to say...

John 8:7 *So when they continued asking Him, He raised Himself up and said to them, "He who is without sin among you, let him throw a stone at her first."*

John 8:8 *And again He stooped down and wrote on the ground.*

John 8:9 *Then those who heard it, being convicted by their conscience, went out one by one, beginning with the oldest even to the last. And Jesus was left alone, and the woman standing in the midst.*

John 8:10 *When Jesus had raised Himself up and saw no one but the woman, He said to her, "Woman, where are those accusers of yours? Has no one condemned you?"*

John 8:11 *She said, "No one, Lord." And Jesus said to her, "Neither do I condemn you; go and sin no more."*

John 8:12 *Then Jesus spoke to them again, saying, "I am the LIGHT of the world. He who follows Me shall not walk in darkness, but have the light of life."* NKJV

Here we see Jesus *showing love* toward the woman taken in adultery, and *shining the light* and exposing the sin of those who stood in judgement over her, before He turns to her and says *"go and sin no more"*.

Only then does He go on to reveal that He is *'the light of the world'*, and in doing so, shows us what the *true purpose* of that *light* is, and that is to expose the sins of those who would set themselves as judges over others, trying hurt, instead of help.

---

21   2 Cor 11:13-15 *For such are false apostles, deceitful workers, transforming themselves into apostles of Christ. And no wonder! For Satan himself transforms himself into an angel of light. Therefore it is no great thing if his ministers also transform themselves into ministers of righteousness, whose end will be according to their works.* NKJV

Light without love can be merciless and cruel. Therefore, you need *love* in order to know *where*, and *what*, to shine the *light* on. That's why satan, in all his deception, can only come as an angel of *light*, never an angel of *love*.

Chapter 2

THE COMMANDMENT TO LOVE

❧ God Is Love

Love is the universal language.

It is instantly understood by all, regardless of age, gender, race, nationality, colour or creed.

It is no surprise then that the apostle John writes in 1st John chapter 4, verses 8 and 16, that 'GOD IS LOVE'[22], and goes on to elaborate in the latter half of verse 16…

> **1 John 4:16b** GOD IS LOVE ('agape':G26); and he that dwelleth in LOVE dwelleth in God, and God in him.[KJV]

MacArthur, in his commentary, states that this is 'God's own description of Himself' and goes on to say that it is 'the most blessed manifestation of the character of God'[23].

---

22   **1 John 4:8** He that loveth not knoweth not God; for God is love.[KJV]

23   John F. MacArthur, *The MacArthur New Testament Commentary, 1 Corinthians,* copyright © 1984 by The Moody Bible Institute of Chicago, p.327

❤ *A New Commandment*

However, this *love* is not just limited to *who*, and *what* God *is*, but it is the kind of love that Jesus *commands* us to walk in, in John chapter 13, verses 34 and 35, where He says…

John 13:34 *A new commandment I give unto you, That ye love one another; As I have loved you, that ye also love one another.*

John 13:35 *By this shall all men know that ye are my disciples, if ye have love ('agape':G26) one to another.* ᴷᴶⱽ

Notice again, that this is a *commandment*, not a *choice*; It applies to every one of us, since we are all now God's children[24], and by extension, His disciples; In other words, whether we *feel like it* or *not*, this is what we are *expected* to do.

Now, there are two key passages of Scripture that deal with this *God-kind of love*. The first is found in Galatians chapter 5, verses 22 and 23, where the apostle Paul writes…

Gal 5:22 *But the fruit (singular, indicating a single fruit) of the Spirit is love' (what follows are the outworking and result of walking in love; they are:) joy, peace, patience, kindness, goodness, faithfulness,*

Gal 5:23 *gentleness and self-control. Against such things there is no law.* ᴺᴵⱽ

We'll be looking at these verses in a little more detail at the end of this study.

The second passage, which is the main focus of this study, is found in 1ˢᵗ Corinthians chapter 13, verses 4 through 8, where the apostle Paul writes…

---

24   *1 John 3:2 Dear friends, now we are children of God, and what we will be has not yet been made known. But we know that when he appears, we shall be like him, for we shall see him as he is.* ᴺᴵⱽ

1 **Cor 13:4** Love suffers long, and is kind; love does not envy; love does
not parade itself, is not puffed up,

1 **Cor 13:5** Does not behave rudely, does not seek its own, is not provoked, thinks no evil;

1 **Cor 13:6** Does not rejoice in iniquity, but rejoices in the truth;

1 **Cor 13:7** Bears all things, believes all things, hopes all things, endures all things.

1 **Cor 13:8a** Love never fails. ᴺᴷᴶⱽ

Now, since God IS love, we could easily substitute 'God' for 'love'
in the above Scripture and get some tremendous insights into
what God is like.

For example "God suffers long, and is kind; God does not envy;
God does not parade Himself, is not puffed up, Does not behave
rudely, does not seek His own, is not provoked, thinks no evil; Does
not rejoice in iniquity, but rejoices in the truth; Bears all things, believes all things, hopes all things, endures all things. God never fails."
[1 Corinthians 13:4-8a]ᴺᴷᴶⱽ

Now we can understand why Matthew chapter 22, verses 35
through 40 says…

Mat 22:35 Then one of them, a lawyer, asked Him a question, testing
Him, and saying,

Mat 22:36 "Teacher, which is the great commandment in the law?"

Mat 22:37 Jesus said to him, " 'You shall love (agapao:G25) the
LORD your God with all your heart, with all your soul, and with
all your mind.'

Mat 22:38 "THIS IS THE FIRST AND GREAT
COMMANDMENT.

Mat 22:39 *"And the second is like it: 'You shall love your neighbour as yourself.'*

Mat 22:40 *"On these two commandments hang all the Law and the Prophets."* NKJV

♥ The Royal Law

Jesus understood the importance of love. He not only descended from God, but *was* Himself God according to John chapter 1, verses 1 and 14[25].

And since He was God, and *'God is love'*, then we know that Jesus was Himself, love *'manifested in the flesh'*.

Also since the entire Old Testament (which consists of *the Law* and *the Prophets*) came from *Love*, that's why Jesus says that it can all be simplified down to *two commandments* (not *choices*): first, *Love God*, and second, *love your neighbour*.

The apostle James picked up on this and called love *'the Royal Law'*, and wrote in James chapter 2 and verse 8…

James 2:8 *If ye fulfil the ROYAL LAW according to the scripture, Thou shalt LOVE (agapao:G25) thy neighbour as thyself, ye do well:* KJV

Added to this the apostle Paul himself wrote in Galatians chapter 5 and verse 14…

Gal 5:14 *For ALL THE LAW is fulfilled in ONE WORD, even in this; Thou shalt LOVE (agapao:G25) thy neighbour as thyself.* KJV

In fact, just previous to this, in **Galatians 5:6**, Paul had just finished saying that *"The only thing that counts is FAITH express-*

---

25 **John 1:1,14a** *In the beginning was the Word, and the Word was with God, and the Word was God.* [14] *And the Word became flesh and dwelt among us,* NKJV

ing itself through LOVE.[NIV]", and substantiated it by saying in 1st Corinthians 13:2…

1 Cor 13:2b *…and if I have ALL FAITH, so as to remove MOUN-TAINS, but do not have LOVE ('agape':G26), I AM NOTH-ING.* [NASB]

In other words, *nothing* you do *outside* of love pleases God, even faith.

That's why we are told to *pursue love* in 1st Corinthians 14:1, to *put on love* in Colossians 3:14, to *increase and abound in love* in 1st Thessalonians 3:12, to *be sincere in love* in 2nd Corinthians 8:8, to *be unified in love* in Philippians 2:2, to *be fervent in love* in 1st Peter 4:8, and to *stimulate one another to love* in Hebrews 10:24.[26]

That being the case, it is *essential* that we find out *exactly what* it is, and *how* we are to walk in it.

♥ A More Excellent Way

Now, as a lead up to 1st Corinthians 13, the great love chapter, Paul concludes chapter 12 by saying in verse 31…

1 Cor 12:31 *But earnestly desire the best gifts ('best' for the office you stand in[27], and the needs at the time). And (he goes on to say…) yet I show you a more excellent way.* [NKJV]

The reason that Paul calls love '*a more excellent way*' is because

---

26   John F. MacArthur, *The MacArthur New Testament Commentary, 1 Corinthians*, copyright © 1984 by The Moody Bible Institute of Chicago, p.330

27   It is important that you earnestly desire (or '*covet earnestly*') the gifts (or manifestations) that will enhance what God wants to do through the office (apostle, prophet, evangelist, pastor-teacher) He has called you to, so that you can bless, and bring more people into the kingdom of God: *For example the evangelist should covet miracles and healings; the prophet should covet earnestly word of wisdom, word of knowledge and prophecy, etc.*

moving in the gifts have *nothing* to do with spirituality or maturity, only *availability*.

Spirituality and *maturity* require *love*, which takes *time spent* in the *Word of God* (to both *hear* and *do*), and time spent *fellowshipping* with God, which is why it is considered 'a more excellent way'.

The word 'way' in the Greek means 'road' or 'highway', referring to the public roads that the Greeks built to benefit everyone, in place of the dirt tracks that people used to build that only benefited themselves.

And the point that Paul was making was that, without a foundation of *love*, all you'll do with the *gifts* is build a road for yourself, *not* to bless others with, but to make a name for yourself, and look good in front of others.

Therefore, in order for God to use you in *the gifts of the Spirit*, and *continue* to do so, you must not only *operate* in *love*, but also let *love* be your *primary motivation* for moving in the *gifts*, which is why Paul goes on to say in the next verse, in 1st Corinthians 13:1...

1 **Cor 13:1** *Though I speak with the tongues of men and of angels, but have not LOVE, I have become sounding brass or a clanging cymbal (something that makes no musical sound, but designed to make loud noises in order to draw attention to itself).* NKJV

Again, we see here that, *speaking in tongues* and *moving in the gifts* don't make you *spiritual* – only your *motive*, and that's *love*.

And as to the word 'love' itself, it's *the same word* that's used in 1st John 4, verses 8 and 16, to describe God.

❧ A LOOK AT THE GOD-KIND OF LOVE

In the Greek, it's the *highest form of love* that exists, and in order for us to understand what it really means, we need to be aware that, unlike the English language that has only one word to describe love in all of it's various forms, the Greeks have four.

Therefore, it would do us good to see what they are, so that we can get a better idea of the kind of love that 1ˢᵗ John 4, and 1ˢᵗ Corinthians 13 is talking about, and using to describe God.

In ascending order, the first is '*Eros*'. It is best described as '*physical, sexual love*', and it is where we get the English word '*erotic*' from.

Second, there is '*Storge*'. This word is used to describe '*family love*' or '*the love between parents and children*'. It is used only twice[28] in Scripture, and both times *negatively*.

Third, there is '*Phileo*', used *over 26 times* in Scripture, ranging in meaning from '*friendship*'[29] to '*tender, affectionate love*'[30] and can be best understood by it's use in John 5:20, with Jesus using it to describe His Father's love toward Him, saying...

John 5:20a *For the Father LOVES (phileo:G5368) the Son and shows Him all He does.* ᴺᴵⱽ

The Fourth word for love, and the highest kind that exists, is '*Agape-Love*'. That's the word used to describe Who God *IS*, and the kind of love that *we* are *commanded* to walk in according to 1ˢᵗ Corinthians 13.

It is so rich in meaning that it took the apostle Paul fifteen different '*words*' or '*qualities*' to try and describe it, each of which we will be looking at in detail over the next several chapters.

---

28   Romans 1:31, 2ⁿᵈ Timothy 3:3.

29   *QuickVerse – Strong's Exhaustive Concordance Of The Bible*, James Strong. Macdonald Publishing Company, Mclean, Virginia. (*Software Version*)

30   *QuickVerse – Strong's Exhaustive Concordance Of The Bible*, James Strong. Macdonald Publishing Company, Mclean, Virginia. (*Software Version*)

❤ *A Love Of The Heart, Soul & Mind*

As we look at these qualities, it is important to note that *Agape-love* is not just the love of *will*, or *choice*, but a love that *'proceeds from the heart that is charitable and unselfish'*, which is why Romans 5:5 says that…

Rom 5:5b …*THE LOVE OF GOD is shed abroad IN OUR HEARTS (where 'feelings' proceed from) by the Holy Ghost which is given unto us.* KJV

Added to this, Jesus said in Matthew 22:33…

Mat 22:37b …*Thou shalt LOVE the Lord thy God with ALL thy HEART, and with ALL thy SOUL, and with ALL thy MIND.* KJV

This in itself proves that this love does, in fact, involve *the heart*, and therefore, *is not without feelings*, and why the apostle Peter says in 1ˢᵗ Peter chapter 1 and verse 22…

1 Pet 1:22 *Now that you have purified yourselves by obeying the truth so that you have sincere love for your brothers, LOVE one another deeply, FROM THE HEART.* NIV

Not only this, but the apostle Peter also goes on to say in 2ⁿᵈ Peter chapter 1, verses 5 through 7…

2 Pet 1:5 *And beside this, giving all diligence, ADD to your faith virtue; and to virtue knowledge;*

2 Pet 1:6 *And to knowledge temperance; and to temperance patience; and to patience godliness;*

2 Pet 1:7 *And to godliness brotherly kindness; and to brotherly kindness (or 'Phileo-Love') (we could say in context: ADD) CHARITY (or 'Agape-Love')* KJV

In other words, since *Agape-Love* is built on, and superior to *Phileo-Love*, it must mean that *it has all the feelings of Phileo*, with the added dimension of 'will' and 'determination', to *stop it* from *wavering*, and being *unpredictable*.

And furthermore, every time you exercise it towards your brothers and sisters in the Lord, remember what Jesus said in Matthew chapter 25 and verse 40, and that is…

Mat 25:40 …*Verily I say unto you, Inasmuch as ye have done it unto one of the LEAST of these my brethren, YE HAVE DONE IT UNTO ME.* KJV

What a tremendous blessing that is, to be able to actually love the Lord and bless Him by way of loving and blessing other Christians (for which we'll be rewarded eternally).

♥ The Primary Motivation

Following this, the apostle Paul goes on to say in 1st Corinthians chapter 13 and verse 2…

1 Cor 13:2 *And though I have the gift of prophecy (which Paul is going to say is the best gift in the first four verses of chapter 14, because it is understood by all, and edifies the whole church), and understand all mysteries, and all knowledge; and though I have all faith, so that I could remove mountains (notice that this is plural), and have not LOVE (Agape-love), I am nothing (Gk. 'useless' or 'worthless'[31]).* KJV

In other words, even if you were the most *spiritual, powerful* and *knowledgeable* person on the face of this earth, revered and admired by all, but didn't walk in love, you would be '*nothing*', or

---

31   *QuickVerse – NAS Exhaustive Concordance Of The Bible,* © 1981 by the Lockman
      Foundation, all rights reserved. (*Software Version*)

literally, *useless and worthless* to God. Added to this, verse 3 goes on to say…

1 Cor 13:3 *And though I bestow ALL my goods to feed the poor, and though I give my body to be burned, and have not LOVE (Agape-love), it profiteth me nothing.* KJV

Notice that in the previous verse Paul said '*I AM nothing*', and now in this verse he says '*it PROFITS me nothing*'.

In other words, you can be the biggest giver in the church, giving ALL you have to those in need, and do it for the wrong reasons, and Paul says that you will not profit from it at all.

Simply put, God isn't impressed with your *giving*; He is only impressed with your *motives*. Jesus put it this way, in Matthew chapter 6, verses 1 through 4…

Mat 6:1 *Take heed that ye do not your alms before men, to be seen of them: otherwise ye have no reward of your Father which is in heaven.*

Mat 6:2 *Therefore when thou doest thine alms, do not sound a trumpet before thee, as the hypocrites do in the synagogues and in the streets, that they may have glory of men. Verily I say unto you, They have their reward.*

Mat 6:3 *But when thou doest alms, let not thy left hand know what thy right hand doeth:*

Mat 6:4 *That thine alms may be in secret: and thy Father which seeth in secret Himself shall reward thee openly.* KJV

What's more, according to verse 3, not only does your financial giving mean nothing to God if it's done outside of *love*, but so do *all the other sacrifices* you make, regardless of how *extreme* they may be; And that includes giving your body to be *burned* for your beliefs.

Therefore, it is essential that we learn exactly *how*, and *what* it means to walk in *the God-kind of love*, and *excel* at it.

❤ *An Overview Of What Love Is & What Love Does*

Now as we approach verses 4 through 7, of 1st Corinthians 13, we are going to find that the apostle Paul gives us a *comprehensive* Biblical *description* of the *fullness* of *what love is*, and *what love does*, in the following way:

He begins with 2 of the most *positive*, and *important* things, that *love is*, and that is *patient* and *kind*.

He then goes on to give us a list of 8 things that *love is not*: Namely, it's *not jealous, does not brag, is not arrogant, does not behave badly, does not insist on its own way, does not get angry, does not remember wrongs*, and finally, *does not rejoice in what's wrong*.

Paul then concludes his definition by listing 5 more things that *love does*, and that is, it *rejoices with the truth, bears all things, believes all things, hopes all things*, and finally, *endures all things*, which is why he says in *verse 8,* 'love never fails'.

With all this in mind, let's go on and look at each of these qualities in some detail, one at a time, and see what Jesus really meant when He said in John chapter 13, verses 34 and 35...

John 13:34 A NEW COMMANDMENT I give unto you, That ye LOVE one another; As I have loved you, that ye also love one another.

John 13:35 BY THIS shall ALL MEN KNOW that ye are MY DISCIPLES, IF YE HAVE LOVE ('agape':G26) one to another.
KJV

Chapter 3

LOVE'S PATIENCE & FORGIVENESS

❧ Love Suffers Long

To begin our study on *love*, turn to 1st Corinthians chapter 13, and let's begin in verse 4, where the apostle Paul lists the first *quality*, or *description*, of *what love is*, and says…

1 Cor 13:4a *Love suffers long,* … NKJV

In the Greek, the word translated '*suffers long*' (Gk. '*makrothumeo*') means to be '*patient, forbearing, long-spirited*' or '*long tempered*'[32] (not *short-tempered*) and has to do with '*actual offences and injuries one receives from others*'[33].

It is this quality that stops you from immediately reacting negatively to others, regardless of how unpleasant they may be (or *appear* to be).

It has the ability to be *inconvenienced, offended, injured* or '*taken advantage of*' by a person over and over again and *not* be upset or angry[34].

---

32   John F. MacArthur, *The MacArthur New Testament Commentary, 1 Corinthians*, copyright © 1984 by The Moody Bible Institute of Chicago, p.338

33   Simon J. Kistemaker, *1 Corinthians*, Baker Books, A Division of Baker Book House Co, Grand Rapids, Michigan 49516, July 2002 p.458

34   John F. MacArthur, *The MacArthur New Testament Commentary, 1 Corinthians*, copyright © 1984 by The Moody Bible Institute of Chicago, p.338

Sadly, this quality is greatly lacking in the Body of Christ, with most Christians wanting to do what James and John wanted to do to those that rejected Jesus (and obviously offended them) in Luke chapter 9 and verse 54, where it is written...

Luke 9:54 And when His disciples James and John saw this, they said, "Lord, do You want us to command fire to come down from heaven and consume them, just as Elijah did?"

Luke 9:55 But He turned and rebuked them, and said, "You do not know what manner of spirit you are of.

Luke 9:56 "For the Son of Man did not come to destroy men's lives but to save them." And they went to another village. ᴺᴷᴶⱽ

John F. MacArthur defines 'long-suffering' to be 'the calm willing-ness to accept certain situations that are irritating or painful', and says that it is generally used of a person who is *wronged* and who has it *easily in their power* to avenge themselves, but will never do so[35].

That certainly was the case here with Jesus.

One word from Him, and that entire village would be wiped off the face of the earth. But that's not the way *Love* behaves.

And if we are to please the Lord, we must learn to behave as He did, and not as the disciples did, for which they were *rebuked*.

♥ *The Importance Of Operating In Patient Love*

The apostle Paul understood *the importance* of walking in *patient-love* and said in Romans chapter 12, verses 17 through 19...

Rom 12:17 Do not repay anyone evil for evil. Be careful to do what is right in the eyes of everybody.

---

35   John F. MacArthur, *The MacArthur New Testament Commentary, 1 Corinthians*, copy-right © 1984 by The Moody Bible Institute of Chicago, p.338

Rom 12:18 *If it is possible, as far as it depends on you, live at peace with everyone.*

Rom 12:19 *Do not take revenge, my friends, but leave room for God's wrath, for it is written: "It is mine to avenge; I will repay," says the Lord.* NIV

Jesus Himself teaches us what it means to be patient and long-suffering, in Matthew chapter 5, verses 39 through 48, where he says...

Mat 5:39 *"But I say to you, do not resist him who is evil; but whoever slaps you on your right cheek, turn to him the other also.*

Mat 5:40 *"And if anyone wants to sue you, and take your shirt, let him have your coat also.*

Mat 5:41 *"And whoever shall force you to go one mile, go with him two.*

Mat 5:42 *"Give to him who asks of you, and do not turn away from him who wants to borrow from you.*

Mat 5:43 *"You have heard that it was said, 'YOU SHALL LOVE YOUR NEIGHBOR, and hate your enemy.'*

Mat 5:44 *"But I say to you, love your enemies, and pray for those who persecute you*

Mat 5:45 *in order that you may be sons of your Father who is in heaven; for He causes His sun to rise on the evil and the good, and sends rain on the righteous and the unrighteous.*

Mat 5:46 *"For if you love those who love you, what reward have you? Do not even the tax-gatherers do the same?*

Mat 5:47 "And if you greet your brothers only, what do you do more than others? Do not even the Gentiles do the same?

Mat 5:48 "Therefore you are to be perfect, as your heavenly Father is perfect. NASB

It is *essential* that we all come to the realisation that, even though people are involved, and have a will of their own, our *real enemy* is not simply what we see in front of us, but as Paul puts it in Ephesians chapter 6 and verse 12…

Eph 6:12 For we wrestle NOT against flesh and blood, but against principalities, against powers, against the rulers of the darkness of this world, against spiritual wickedness in high places. KJV

If we don't get this revelation, we will end up fighting each other, break *the commandment of love* given to us by Jesus in John 13:34, and allow the devil to work *unhindered*, without any resistance, whatsoever.

❦ LOVE'S FORGIVENESS

Before we can continue to deal with this very powerful quality of love, we need to jump ahead to the 9th *quality* mentioned in 1st Corinthians 13:5, that is essential to *love's patience and longsuffering,* and that is *forgiveness,* or as Paul put it, *LOVE…*

1 Cor 13:5b ...thinks no evil; NKJV

In the literal Greek, it actually says that '*love does not take into account a wrong suffered*'[36], nor does it '*...keep a record of wrongs*'[37].

The Greek word ('*logizomai*':G3049) for '*account*' is actually a bookkeeping term that means '*to calculate*' or '*reckon*'[38], and makes reference to the kind of detailed, itemised, permanent record that are kept for business purposes, that can be consulted at any time.

And Paul says that we are, most definitely, *not to keep track of the injuries and injustices* committed against us, but that we must be *extremely forgiving and forgetful*, and make sure that we *never mention them again.*

The reason being that, this is exactly what God does with us, according to Romans chapter 4 and verse 8, where the apostle Paul writes...

Rom 4:8 "*Blessed is the man whose sin the Lord will not take into account.*"[NASB]

This is actually a quote from Psalms 32, verses 1 and 2, where David says...

Psa 32:1b *...Blessed is he whose transgressions are forgiven, whose sins are covered.*

Psa 32:2 *Blessed is the man whose sin the LORD DOES NOT COUNT AGAINST HIM and in whose spirit is no deceit.* [NIV]

Added to this, Acts chapter 3 and verse 19 says...

---

36   John F. MacArthur, *The MacArthur New Testament Commentary*, *1 Corinthians*, copyright © 1984 by The Moody Bible Institute of Chicago, p.347

37   Simon J. Kistemaker, *1 Corinthians*, Baker Books, A Division of Baker Book House Co, Grand Rapids, Michigan 49516, July 2002 p.459

38   John F. MacArthur, *The MacArthur New Testament Commentary*, *1 Corinthians*, copyright © 1984 by The Moody Bible Institute of Chicago, p.347

Acts 3:19 *"Repent therefore and return, that your sins may be
WIPED AWAY (KJV - 'BLOTTED OUT'), in order that
times of refreshing may come from the presence of the Lord;* KJV

Therefore, for all those who say that love does not forgive and
forget, but rather remembers and still forgives are wrong; It is *re-
sentment* that *seemingly forgives* but *refuses* to forget.

Love, on the other hand, has no room, nor provision, for remembering wrongs: In fact, *"a wrong done against love is like a
spark that falls into the sea (of forgetfulness) and is quenched"*[39].

To put it another way, love's forgiveness *quenches* wrongs, rather
than *recording* them.

♥ *Forgiveness & Conflict Resolution*

And since God is willing to *forgive us* to the point of *completely
and permanently erasing all record of our sins against Him*[40], then it
is not hard to understand why He expects the same from us, and
why Jesus says in Mark chapter 11, verses 25 and 26...

Mark 11:25 *And when ye stand praying, FORGIVE, if ye have ought
against ANY: that your Father also which is in heaven may forgive
you your trespasses.*

Mark 11:26 *BUT IF YE DO NOT FORGIVE, NEITHER
WILL YOUR FATHER WHICH IS IN HEAVEN FOR-
GIVE YOUR TRESPASSES.* KJV

In short, you must first forgive others of their sin, if you are ever
going to be forgiven of yours; Because, if you don't, you are breaking *the commandment of love*, and are already in sin *yourself.*

39　John F. MacArthur, *The MacArthur New Testament Commentary*, 1 Corinthians, copyright © 1984 by The Moody Bible Institute of Chicago, p.347

40　*Jer 31:34b ...for I will forgive their iniquity, and I will remember their sin no more.* KJV

For the record, if anyone should commit a sin against you, besides forgiving them, the Bible gives very clear instructions on what to do; Jesus Himself teaches us in Matthew chapter 18, beginning in verse 15...

Mat 18:15 *If your brother sins against you, go and show him his fault, just between the two of you. If he listens to you, you have won your brother over.* NIV

In other words, Jesus says, deal with it as quickly as possible and keep it as private as possible, to avoid others knowing about it, and getting needlessly involved in it (both them and their emotions).

However, if your initial efforts don't work, then Jesus goes on to say in verse 16...

Mat 18:16 *But if he will not listen, take one or two others along, so that 'every matter may be established by the testimony of two or three witnesses.'* NIV

The *'one or two others'* that are mentioned here are referring to neutral witnesses, not *your* best friends.

That way, everything remains impartial, and makes it *very easy* for the person in the wrong to make amends (without feeling like they've been *picked on*, and *unfairly treated*).

But if this fails as well, Jesus goes on to give two more instructions in verse 17, and they are...

Mat 18:17 *If he refuses to listen to them, tell it to the church; and if he refuses to listen even to the church, treat him as you would a pagan or a tax collector.* NIV

Therefore, for someone that *refuses* to listen, and *refuses* to repent, Jesus says that the first thing you do is inform the entire church so that they can all get involved, and perhaps one of them may be able to resolve the problem.

But regardless of who is involved in this resolution, the apostle Paul gives very clear instructions as to the attitude it is to be done in; He explains in Galatians chapter 6 and verse 1...

Gal 6:1 *Brethren, if a man be overtaken in a fault, ye which are spiritual, restore such an one in the spirit of meekness; considering thyself, lest thou also be tempted.* KJV

However, if all this fails, Jesus goes on to say, 'treat him as you would a pagan or tax collector', meaning that you need to revert back to the kind of love and care you would show a sinner, in an effort to help them come to God.

❧ Patience & Forgiveness – Two Inseparable Qualities

Now, returning to *forgiveness* and *long-suffering*, the reason that we covered them back-to-back is because of what is brought out in Matthew chapter 18, that relates to *both these qualities*, beginning in verse 21, where it says...

Mat 18:21 *Then came Peter to him, and said, Lord, how oft shall my brother sin against me, and I forgive him? till seven times?* KJV

In New Testament times, the Greeks had greatly influenced the thinking of the time, and a very famous Greek philosopher by the name of Aristotle taught that the great Greek *virtue* was *refusal* to tolerate insult or injury, and to *strike back* in retaliation for the *slightest* offence.

Therefore, *self-sacrificial love* and *non-avenging patience* were considered to be 'weaknesses' and *unworthy* of noble men and women; And for Peter to even suggest forgiveness *seven times* in a day was *extremely* generous[41].

The way we know that it was seven times in a single day is be-

---

41   John F. MacArthur, *The MacArthur New Testament Commentary, 1 Corinthians*, copyright © 1984 by The Moody Bible Institute of Chicago, p.338

cause of what Jesus said in Luke chapter 17 and verse 4, and that is...

Luke 17:4 *And if he trespass against thee seven times in a day, and seven times in a day turn again to thee, saying, I repent; thou shalt forgive him.* KJV

It has always been in *your power* to *forgive*.

Regardless of whether the person asks for forgiveness or not, you must still forgive them. If you are wondering *where to draw the line*, just ask yourself *how far do you want God to go before He draws a line with you?*

As to *the difference* between forgiving someone that *asks* for forgiveness and someone that *doesn't* is that the person that *asks* to be forgiven is *opening the door for fellowship to be restored immediately*, while the other keeps it shut.

This same principle applies to our relationship with God when we sin against Him. As soon as we ask God to forgive us, we *immediately restore fellowship with Him*, and 1ˢᵗ John 1:9 promises us that...

1 John 1:9b *...He is faithful and just to forgive us our sins and to cleanse us from all unrighteousness.* NKJV

Continuing on in Matthew chapter 18, and verse 23, Jesus continues on to say...

Mat 18:23 *Therefore is the kingdom of heaven likened unto a certain king, which would take account of his servants.*

Mat 18:24 *And when he had begun to reckon, one was brought unto him, which owed him ten thousand talents (our closest, conservative estimation of this is about 19 million dollars if it's silver, and 290 million if it's gold).*

Mat 18:25 But forasmuch as he had not to pay, his lord commanded him to be sold, and his wife, and children, and all that he had, and payment to be made.

Mat 18:26 The servant therefore fell down, and worshipped him, saying, Lord, have PATIENCE with me, and I will pay thee all. KJV

And following his servants plea for *patience*, notice that *forgiveness* is the very next thing mentioned in verse 27, where Jesus goes on to say...

Mat 18:27 Then the lord of that servant was moved with compassion, and loosed him, and FORGAVE him the debt. KJV

In other words, this man's multi-million dollar debt has been cancelled in an instant of time; But instead of rejoicing and showing the same love and compassion to others in a similar situation under him, it says in verse 28...

Mat 18:28 But the same servant went out, and found one of his fellowservants, which owed him an hundred pence (about 17 dollars, by the same reckoning as above): and he laid hands on him, and took him by the throat, saying, Pay me that thou owest.

Mat 18:29 And his fellowservant fell down at his feet, and besought him, saying, Have PATIENCE with me, and I will pay thee all.

Mat 18:30 And he would not: but went and cast him into prison, till he should pay the debt. KJV

This is no different to God *forgiving you* of your *million dollar debt of sin,* and you not forgiving your brother's *20 dollar debt of sin* against you.

Just like this servant, you are now *totally debt free,* and *free* to show *the same generosity* toward others who have sinned against you.

To do any less would not only *displease* God, but *anger Him* as well, as Jesus brings out in the next few verses, beginning in verse 31, where Jesus continues...

Mat 18:31 *So when his fellowservants saw what was done, they were very sorry, and came and told unto their lord all that was done.*

Mat 18:32 *Then his lord, after that he had called him, said unto him, O thou wicked servant, I forgave thee all that debt, because thou desiredst me:*

Mat 18:33 *Shouldest not thou also have had compassion on thy fellowservant, even as I had pity on thee?*

Mat 18:34 *And his lord was WROTH, and delivered him to the tormentors, till he should pay all that was due unto him (in short, the debt that was previously forgiven, has been re-instated).*

Mat 18:35 *So likewise shall my heavenly Father DO ALSO UNTO YOU, if ye from your HEARTS forgive not every one his brother their trespasses.* KJV

This is *exactly* what Jesus meant when He said in Mark chapter 11, verses 25 and 26...

Mark 11:25 *And when ye stand praying, FORGIVE, if ye have ought against ANY: that your Father also which is in heaven may forgive you your trespasses.*

Mark 11:26 *BUT IF YE DO NOT FORGIVE, NEITHER WILL YOUR FATHER WHICH IS IN HEAVEN FORGIVE YOUR TRESPASSES.* KJV

God *knows* that no one will *ever* be able to re-pay *the enormous debt that is owed Him* for sending Jesus to the cross, and *redeem-*

ing us all from hell; Which is why Paul writes in 2ⁿᵈ Corinthians chapter 5 and verse 19...

2 Cor 5:19a *For God was in Christ, reconciling the world to himself, no longer counting people's sins against them.* ᴺᴸᵀ

And since He has *forgiven us all equally* of this *massive debt*, He *expects* the *same* of us for all the *lesser debts* we are owed by those around us.

♥ *Being Willing To Forgive*

If you are one of those people that may be experiencing difficulty in this area because of the nature of sin committed against you, understand that all God wants you to do is to be open to it, and allow Him to help you with it.

What He will not tolerate is you *refusing to forgive*, and *totally closing your heart off to it.*

The apostle Paul combined it all and said in Colossians chapter 3, verses 12 through 14...

Col 3:12 *As God's chosen ones, holy and beloved, clothe yourselves with compassion, kindness, humility, meekness, and patience.*

Col 3:13 *Bear with one another and, if anyone has a complaint against another, forgive each other; just as the Lord has forgiven you, so you also must forgive.*

Col 3:14 *Above all, clothe yourselves with love, which binds everything together in perfect harmony.* ᴺᴿˢⱽ

Paul isn't telling us anything that he himself hasn't already done; In 2ⁿᵈ Corinthians chapter 6, verses 4 through 6, he says...

2 Cor 6:4 *In everything we do we try to show that we are true ministers of God. We patiently endure troubles and hardships and calamities of every kind.*

2 Cor 6:5 *We have been beaten, been put in jail, faced angry mobs, worked to exhaustion, endured sleepless nights, and gone without food.*

2 Cor 6:6 *We have proved ourselves by our purity, our understanding, our patience, our kindness, our sincere love, and the power of the Holy Spirit.* NLT

It's time that we did the same, and learned to walk in *patience and forgiveness*, and *be* the witnesses that God *needs us to be*, in order to *help bring people to Christ*.

Let me finish with a true story from John F. MacArthur's commentary on this quality, that we can all reflect on, and think about, in relation to what we've just learned. He says…

One of Abraham Lincoln's earliest political enemies was Edwin M. Stanton.

He called Lincoln a "low cunning clown" and "the original gorilla".

"It was ridiculous for people to go to Africa to see a gorilla," he would say, "when they could find one easily in Springfield, Illinois."

Lincoln never responded to the slander, but when, as president, he needed a secretary of war, he chose Stanton.

When his sceptical, unbelieving friends asked 'why?', Lincoln replied, "Because he is the best man."

Years later, as the slain president's body lay in state, Stanton looked into the coffin and said through his tears, "There lies the greatest ruler of men the world has ever seen."

His animosity was finally broken by Lincoln's long-suffering, non-retaliatory spirit.

Patient, forgiving, forbearing love won out.[42]

---

42   *1ˢᵗ Cor. 13:8 Love never fails.* NKJV

Chapter 4

LOVE'S KINDNESS

❦ EXPRESSIONS OF KINDNESS

Returning to 1ˢᵗ Corinthians 13 and verse 4, the apostle Paul says there again that...

1 Cor 13:4 Love suffers long, and is kind;... ᴺᴷᴶⱽ

The *kindness* that is spoken of here is *not* the same one that is used *interchangeably* in the Old Testament for mercy and kindness, but specifically refers to the type of kindness that is tender-hearted, that expresses itself in both 'word' and 'deed'.

The apostle Paul writes, in Ephesians chapter 4 and verse 32...

Eph 4:32 (And) be kind to one another, tender-hearted, forgiving each other, just as God in Christ also has forgiven you. ᴺᴬˢᴮ

MacArthur says, *"Just as patience will take anything from others, kindness will give anything to others, even to its enemies. Being kind is the counterpart of being patient."*⁴³

---

43   John F. MacArthur, *The MacArthur New Testament Commentary, 1 Corinthians,* copyright © 1984 by The Moody Bible Institute of Chicago, p.334

If Christians would just operate in *patience, kindness* and *forgiveness,* the world would be a different place today.

People would be *continually blessing others, forgetting the wrongs committed against them* and walking in the *peace* and *joy* God intended for them to walk in all the days of their life; What a *tremendous witness* this would be to the world.

However, it is also true that, as we grow in the *knowledge* and *wisdom* of the Word of God, it won't be long before the *glorious church* will begin to emerge, and *all this will become a reality* in the Body of Christ, to the glory of God.

One of the best examples of kindness in the Bible is the story of the Good Samaritan, found in Luke chapter 10, verses 25 through 37. It reads...

Luke 10:25 *One day an expert in religious law stood up to test Jesus by asking him this question: "Teacher, what must I do to receive eternal life?"*

Luke 10:26 *Jesus replied, "What does the law of Moses say? How do you read it?"*

Luke 10:27 *The man answered, "'You must love the Lord your God with all your heart, all your soul, all your strength, and all your mind.' And, 'Love your neighbour as yourself.'"*

Luke 10:28 *"Right!" Jesus told him. "Do this and you will live!"*

Luke 10:29 *The man wanted to justify his actions, so he asked Jesus, "And who is my neighbour?"*

Luke 10:30 *Jesus replied with an illustration: "A Jewish man was travelling on a trip from Jerusalem to Jericho, and he was attacked by bandits. They stripped him of his clothes and money, beat him up, and left him half dead beside the road.*

Luke 10:31 *"By chance a Jewish priest came along; but when he saw the man lying there, he crossed to the other side of the road and passed him by.*

Luke 10:32 *A Temple assistant walked over and looked at him lying there, but he also passed by on the other side.*

Luke 10:33 *"Then a despised Samaritan came along, and when he saw the man, he felt deep pity.*

Luke 10:34 *Kneeling beside him, the Samaritan soothed his wounds with medicine and bandaged them. Then he put the man on his own donkey and took him to an inn, where he took care of him.*

Luke 10:35 *The next day he handed the innkeeper two pieces of silver and told him to take care of the man. 'If his bill runs higher than that,' he said, 'I'll pay the difference the next time I am here.'*

Luke 10:36 *"Now which of these three would you say was a neighbour to the man who was attacked by bandits?" Jesus asked.*

Luke 10:37 *The man replied, "The one who showed him mercy." Then Jesus said, "Yes, now go and DO the same."* NLT

♥ The Law Of Kindness – Governing What You Say

Kindness is *love in action:* Just as much as *faith* requires *action,* so does *love.*

In the Greek, to be 'kind' (Gk.'*chresteuomai*':G5541) means 'to be *useful, serving and gracious*'; It is active goodwill. It not only FEELS generous, it IS generous. It not only DESIRES others' welfare, but WORKS *for it.*[44]

---

44 John F. MacArthur, *The MacArthur New Testament Commentary, 1 Corinthians,* copyright © 1984 by The Moody Bible Institute of Chicago, p.334

Now, added to good works, which we'll look at in just a moment, Proverbs chapter 31 and verse 26 also shows that *kindness* can be expressed in another way; It says…

Prov 31:26 *She openeth her mouth with wisdom; and in her tongue is the law of KINDNESS.* KJV

In other words, not only does the virtuous woman *deal kindly* with all those around her, but she also *instructs* them with *loving-kindness* as well.

Matthew Henry, in his commentary writes, "*the Law of Loving-Kindness is written in the heart, but it shows itself in the tongue, by what we speak*".

Therefore, if you really love someone with the *God-kind of love*, you will always make the effort to *speak well of them*, regardless of whether or not they *deserve* it.

For those that were having issues with this, the apostle James says, in James chapter 3 and verse 10…

James 3:10 *Out of the same mouth proceed blessing and cursing. My brethren, these things ought not to be so.* NKJV

Also, in terms of *ministering to others*, Jesus said in Matthew chapter 11, verses 28 through 30…

Mat 11:28 *"Come to Me, all who are weary and heavy-laden, and I will give you rest.*

Mat 11:29 *"Take My yoke upon you, and learn from Me, for I am gentle and humble in heart; and you shall find rest for your souls.*

Mat 11:30 *"For My yoke is easy (Gk. 'chrestos':G5543 – meaning 'easy and kind'[45]), and My burden is light."* NASB mod.

---

45   *QuickVerse – Strong's Exhaustive Concordance Of The Bible*, The Hebrew and Greek Dictionary is extracted from *Strong's Exhaustive Concordance Of The Bible*, © copyrighted 1980, 1986 and assigned to World Bible Publishers, Inc. All rights reserved.

The way Jesus ministered to others was *gently* and *kindly*, with all *humbleness of heart*, to where people around Him found *'rest'* for their souls;

And that's the same thing that is expected of us, according the apostle Paul in 2nd Timothy chapter 2, verses 24 and 25, where he writes…

2 Tim 2:24 *And the Lord's servant must not be quarrelsome but kindly to everyone, an apt teacher, patient,*

2 Tim 2:25a *correcting opponents with gentleness.* ^KJV

As to why we are to do this, Paul says in Romans chapter 2 and verse 4…

Rom 2:4 *Or do you think lightly of the riches of His kindness and for-bearance and patience, not knowing that the kindness of God leads you to repentance?* ^NASB

It's sad the number of opportunities we have missed to *minister the Gospel* through *simple expressions of kindness* (in *word* or *deed*), because we were too busy looking for the *winning argument*, that rarely did any good, or saved anyone.

♥ Kindness As Active Good Will

Now, in relation to kindness as *'good works'* or *'active good will'*, Jesus says in Matthew chapter 5 and verse 40…

Mat 5:40 *"And if anyone wants to sue you, and take your shirt, let him have your coat also.*^NASB

In other words, when Jesus said to *'love your enemies'*, He wasn't just telling us to *feel kindly* about them, but to *be kind* to them;

Even to the point where, if all you had was a shirt and coat and someone wanted them, He says, *let them have it.*

At the time this was written, it was unheard of to ask this of anyone, because the legal system did not allow a poor person's outer cloak (or coat) to be taken, since it was their *only* means of protection from the *outside elements*, and *the cold of night.*

Therefore, if by some chance a creditor was to take possession of a person's coat, and they complained about it, it would be returned to them *immediately, without question.*

And it is to this type of situation that Jesus says that we must be *willing* to give up *everything* if necessary, in order to avoid taking action that would *only benefit ourselves.*

However, when it comes to looking after, and protecting what is others, then it's an entirely different story; To that Jesus said in Matthew 25:23...

Mat 25:23 *His lord said unto him, Well done, good and faithful servant; thou hast been faithful over a few things, I will make thee ruler over many things: enter thou into the joy of thy lord.* KJV

Returning to Matthew 5, if what Jesus said previously wasn't hard enough, He goes on to say in verse 41...

Mat 5:41 *"And whoever shall force you to go one mile, go with him two.* NASB

In those days, Roman soldiers had the *legal right* to *force* local residents to carry their back pack for *'one mile'.* At the end of that mile, the person that was forced into doing this duty would throw the pack to the ground, spit on it, and walk away.

However, Jesus says that *loving-kindness* doesn't behave that way; It actually does something totally unexpected, and offers to go *a second mile.*

What's significant about this is that, *the first mile has your adversary in control over you,* while the second mile has *you in control,* since you are *no longer under obligation to do it, and so give you the upper –hand and advantage over him.*

Doing good only to those that are good to you doesn't count for very much, which is why Jesus goes on to say in verse 46…

Mat 5:46 If you love those who love you, what reward will you get? Are not even the tax collectors doing that? KJV

Jews hated to hear this because, not only did tax collectors re- mind them that they were under Roman rule every time they paid taxes, but it was common practice for tax collectors to over charge people, and literally, steal from them.

But worse than a Roman tax collector, was a Jewish tax collec- tor; They were seen as traitors, because they were stealing from their own people, and working for the oppressors, making them the lowest of all in the eyes of the Jews.

With this in mind, Jesus was essentially saying, if you only love those that love you, you are no better than those *you consider* the *lowliest* of all; He goes on to conclude in verses 47 and 48 with…

Mat 5:47 And if you greet only your brothers, what are you doing more than others? Do not even pagans do that?

Mat 5:48 Be perfect, therefore, as your heavenly Father is perfect. NIV

In short, Jesus is saying that it doesn't take much to love those who love you, but it does take *godly loving-kindness* to love those who *don't* love you, and *want* to do you harm; Sometimes, it may mean that you keep your distance, but you are still to love them.

Selfish people live their lives based on *"What's in it for me?"*; Loving-kindness however, looks to bless others, asking the ques- tion, *"What can I do for you?"*

In Hebrews chapter 13 and verse 16, the writer of Hebrews says…

Heb 13:16 Do not neglect to DO GOOD and to share what you have, for such sacrifices are pleasing to God. ^{NRSV}

Notice that *sharing* goes right along with *doing good*; And in the times we live in, there seems to be *ample, unlimited opportunities* to walk in this type of *loving-kindness* toward others; In fact, the apostle Peter said, in 1st Peter chapter 2 and verse 12...

1 Pet 2:12 Live such good lives among the pagans that, though they accuse you of doing wrong, they may see your good deeds and glorify God on the day He visits us. ^{NIV}

In other words, it is your *good deeds* that point to God, not your *good arguments*; This is further confirmed by what Paul wrote to Titus, in Titus chapter 2, verses 7 and 8, where he says...

Titus 2:7 in all things show yourself to be an example of good deeds, with purity in doctrine, dignified,

Titus 2:8 sound in speech which is beyond reproach (meaning that none of it promotes arguments or strife), in order that the opponent may be put to shame, having nothing bad to say about us. ^{NASB}

What's interesting is that, the verses we love to quote so much in Word of Faith circles actually has to do with showing love through acts of kindness, not just words: the apostle James writes in James chapter 2, verses 14 through 16...

James 2:14 What good is it, my brothers, if a man claims to have faith but has no deeds? Can such faith save him?

James 2:15 Suppose a brother or sister is without clothes and daily food.

James 2:16 If one of you says to him, "Go, I wish you well; keep warm and well fed," but does nothing about his physical needs, what good is it?

James 2:17 In the same way, faith by itself, if it is not accompanied by action, is dead. NIV

In other words, the apostle James tells us that, *not only* does faith *demand* action, but *so does love;* Especially when it's *difficult.* That's where *the reward* is, and why Jesus says in Luke chapter 6 and verse 35...

Luke 6:35 But love your enemies, do good, and lend, expecting nothing in return. Your reward will be great, and you will be children of the Most High; for He is kind to the ungrateful and the wicked. NRSV

♥ *How Will You Be Remembered?*

Many times, *you are remembered* for your *good deeds*, not just your character or personality; That was certainly the case with Tabitha in Acts chapter 9 and verse 36, where it is written...

Acts 9:36 Now there was at Joppa a certain disciple named Tabitha, which by interpretation is called Dorcas: this woman was full of (or 'abounding with' NASB*) good works (which the New American Standard Bible refers to as 'deeds of kindness'* NASB*) and almsdeeds which she did.* KJV

The New Living Translation says that, *"She was always doing kind things for others and helping the poor."*

This is one of the *basic functions of Christianity*, or being a child of God, and that is *'doing good';* That's why Paul said in Galatians chapter 6, verses 9 and 10...

Gal 6:9 *And let us not be weary in well doing: for in due season we shall reap, if we faint not.*

Gal 6:10 *As we have therefore opportunity, let us do good (or 'be kind' *[TLB]*) unto all men, especially unto them who are of the household of faith.* [KJV]

One aspect of 'doing good', and therefore 'being kind', that is often overlooked is what is brought out in Acts chapter 10 and verse 38, where the Bible says...

Acts 10:38 *How God anointed Jesus of Nazareth with the Holy Ghost and with power: Who went about doing good, and healing all that were oppressed of the devil; for God was with him.* [KJV]

A part of our *loving-kindness* is to include '*healing all that are oppressed of the devil*'; Not to just *feel* sorry for them; And that's a part of what 1st Corinthians 13:4 means when it says that '*Agape-Love is Kind*'.

Loving-kindness is essential to the Body of Christ; It is something that, as we are led by the Spirit, will *set us apart from the rest of the world.*

To conclude this particular quality, I'd like to relate to you the following story:

William Gladstone, a prime minister of England in the nineteenth century, one night was working late on an important speech he was to give to the House of Commons the next day.

At about two o'clock in the morning a woman knocked on his door, asking the servant if Mr. Gladstone would come and comfort her young crippled son who lay dying in a tenement not far away.

Without hesitation the busy man set his speech aside and went.

He told a friend later that morning, "I am the happiest man in the world today".

The true greatness of Gladstone was not in his political position or attainments but in his great love, a love that would risk his political future to show the love of Christ to a young boy in great need.

As it turned out, that morning he also made what some historians claim was the greatest speech of his life.

He gained that victory, too, but he had been willing to loose it for the sake of a greater victory.

Love's victory was more important.[46]

It doesn't *take* a lot to *do* a lot; Just a *kind heart,* and an *open hand* that is sensitive to *the Spirit's leading.*

---

46   John F. MacArthur, *The MacArthur New Testament Commentary, 1 Corinthians,* copy-
     right © 1984 by The Moody Bible Institute of Chicago, p.351

Chapter 5

LOVE – NOT ENVIOUS OR JEALOUS

✵ Love Does Not Envy

Returning to 1st Corinthians chapter 13 and verse 4, the apostle Paul says there again...

1 Cor 13:4 *Love suffers long, and is kind; (and goes on to add...) love does not envy;* NKJV

The Greek word for '*envy*' (Gk. '*zeloo*':G2206) actually means '*to be jealous*' or '*have a strong desire*'[47].

It is said to be '*the enemy of honour*' (getting upset and angry when others receive recognition), and '*the sorrow of fools*' (*feeling sorry* for themselves when they aren't in the spotlight).

The *eye* is both the *inlet* and *outlet* of this particular sin. That's why 1st Samuel chapter 18 and verse 9 reads the way it does, and says...

1 Sam 18:9 *And from that time on Saul kept a jealous eye on David.* NIV

---

47   John F. MacArthur, *The MacArthur New Testament Commentary, 1 Corinthians*, copyright © 1984 by The Moody Bible Institute of Chicago, p.340

Proverbs chapter 27 and verse 4 *warns us about jealousy* and says...

Prov 27:4 *Wrath is fierce and anger is a flood, But who can stand before jealousy?* [NASB]

In other words, *jealousy* is *not* a *moderate* or *harmless sin*; It is about *possession* and *control*; Therefore, it is *extremely dangerous*, and sometimes even *deadly*. The apostle James understood this and wrote in James chapter 4, verses 1 through 3...

James 4:1 *What is causing the quarrels and fights among you? Isn't it the whole army of evil desires at war within you?*

James 4:2 *You want what you don't have, so you scheme and kill to get it. (James now identifies one of these 'evil desires' and says...) You are jealous (Gk. 'zeloo':G2206) for what others have, and you can't possess it, so you fight and quarrel to take it away from them. And yet the reason you don't have what you want is that you don't ask God for it.*

James 4:3 *And even when you do ask, you don't get it because your whole motive is wrong--you want only what will give you pleasure.* NLT mod.

It was *envy and jealousy* that resulted in Joseph's brothers selling him into slavery, and Daniel being thrown into the lions den, and why the apostle James had already said previously in James chapter 3, verses 14 through 16...

James 3:14 *But if you have bitter jealousy and selfish ambition in your heart, do not be arrogant and so lie against the truth.*

James 3:15 *This wisdom is not that which comes down from above, but is earthly, natural, demonic.*

James 3:16 For where jealousy and selfish ambition exist, there is disorder and every evil thing. [NASB]

The apostle Paul had some experience with this while he was in prison and wrote in Philippians chapter 1, verses 15 through 19…

Phil 1:15 Some proclaim Christ from envy and rivalry, but others from goodwill.

Phil 1:16 These proclaim Christ out of love, knowing that I have been put here for the defense of the gospel;

Phil 1:17 the others proclaim Christ out of selfish ambition, not sincerely but intending to increase my suffering in my imprisonment.

Phil 1:18 What does it matter? Just this, that Christ is proclaimed in every way, whether out of false motives or true; and in that I rejoice. Yes, and I will continue to rejoice,

Phil 1:19 for I know that through your prayers and the help of the Spirit of Jesus Christ this will turn out for my deliverance. [NRSV]

Paul refused to return *envy for envy*; Instead, he was just glad that the Gospel was being preached, regardless of *who* did it, and *why*.

♥ Jealousy That Covets What Is Others

Jealousy comes in two forms: The first kind says, "*I want what someone else has*", and that can be anything from a car, to a house, to being recognised at work, not because what they have isn't any good, but because it's not *as* good.

In fact, some even go as far as to say, "*I wish they didn't have what they have*"; That was the case in Matthew chapter 20, when the labourers hired at the beginning of the day were paid the *same wage* as those hired at the end of the day, and it says in verse 11...

Mat 20:11 And when they received it, they grumbled against the landowner,

Mat 20:12 saying, 'These last worked only one hour, and you have made them equal to us who have borne the burden of the day and the scorching heat.'

Mat 20:13 But he replied to one of them, 'Friend, I am doing you no wrong; did you not agree with me for the usual daily wage?

Mat 20:14 Take what belongs to you and go; I choose to give to this last the same as I give to you.

Mat 20:15 Am I not allowed to do what I choose with what belongs to me? Or are you ENVIOUS because I am GENEROUS?'

Mat 20:16 So the last will be first, and the first will be last." NRSV

♥ *Jealousy That Desires Evil For Others*

The *second type* of jealousy is both *selfish* and *dangerous*, and *desires evil* for others.

Solomon encountered this type of jealousy in one of the two women that came to him in 1st Kings chapter 3, verses 16 through 28, where it says...

1 Ki 3:16 Later, two women who were prostitutes came to the king and stood before him.

1 Ki 3:17 The one woman said, "Please, my lord, this woman and I live in the same house; and I gave birth while she was in the house.

1 *Ki* 3:18 *Then on the third day after I gave birth, this woman also gave birth. We were together; there was no one else with us in the house, only the two of us were in the house.*

1 *Ki* 3:19 *Then this woman's son died in the night, because she lay on him.*

1 *Ki* 3:20 *She got up in the middle of the night and took my son from beside me while your servant slept. She laid him at her breast, and laid her dead son at my breast.*

1 *Ki* 3:21 *When I rose in the morning to nurse my son, I saw that he was dead; but when I looked at him closely in the morning, clearly it was not the son I had borne."*

1 *Ki* 3:22 *But the other woman said, "No, the living son is mine, and the dead son is yours." The first said, "No, the dead son is yours, and the living son is mine." So they argued before the king.*

1 *Ki* 3:23 *Then the king said, "The one says, 'This is my son that is alive, and your son is dead'; while the other says, 'Not so! Your son is dead, and my son is the living one.'"*

1 *Ki* 3:24 *So the king said, "Bring me a sword," and they brought a sword before the king.*

1 *Ki* 3:25 *The king said, "Divide the living boy in two; then give half to the one, and half to the other."*

1 *Ki* 3:26 *But the woman whose son was alive said to the king--because compassion for her son burned within her--" Please, my lord, give her the living boy; certainly do not kill him!" The other said, "It shall be neither mine nor yours; divide it."*

1 *Ki* 3:27 *Then the king responded: "Give the first woman the living boy; do not kill him. She is his mother."* NRSV

In *absolute contrast* to this, and the only *positive aspect* of jealousy I've found, is that which is brought out in Deuteronomy chapter 4, verses 23 and 24, where it says...

Deu 4:23 *Be careful not to forget the covenant of the LORD your God that he made with you; do not make for yourselves an idol in the form of anything the LORD your God has forbidden.*

Deu 4:24 *For the LORD your God is a consuming fire, a jealous God.* NIV

God's *jealousy*, or *'strong desire'*, proceeds from *His love for His people*, that they only ever have *the very best*, and *nothing less*.

But as for the rest of us, as *Dale Burke*[48] put it, *"jealousy is the best way to get rid of what you're afraid of losing"*;

He goes on to say, *"When I reject jealousy, I choose to trust another person. When I reject envy, I choose to trust God."*

Jealousy is *grief* to ourselves, *anger* towards God, and *ill-will* to our neighbour. It is a *sin* without *pleasure*, *profit* or *honour*.

---

48   H. Dale Burke, *A Love That Never Fails: 1 Corinthians 13*, © 1999 by H. Dale Burke and Jac La Tour, Moody Press, Chicago. P.46,48

Chapter 6

LOVE DOES NOT BRAG OR BOAST

❧ Boasting & Bragging – The Other Side Of Jealousy

Returning again to 1st Corinthians 13 and verse 4, Paul writes...

1 Cor 13:4a *Love suffers long, and is kind; love does not envy; love does not parade itself...* NKJV

The Greek word for *'parade'* (Gk.'*perpereuomai*':G4068) means *'to brag, boast*[49], *or talk conceitedly*[50]; *to have an exaggerated opinion of yourself.'*

Therefore, what Paul is saying here is that *'love does not boast, brag, or have an exaggerated opinion of itself – parading its accomplishments for all to see'.*

Boasting and bragging is the other side of *jealousy:* MacArthur says that *"Jealousy is wanting what someone else has; Bragging is try-*

---

49 *QuickVerse – Strong's Exhaustive Concordance Of The Bible*, The Hebrew and Greek Dictionary is extracted from *Strong's Exhaustive Concordance Of The Bible*, © copyrighted 1980, 1986 and assigned to World Bible Publishers, Inc. All rights reserved.

50 John F. MacArthur, *The MacArthur New Testament Commentary, 1 Corinthians*, copyright © 1984 by The Moody Bible Institute of Chicago, p.341

ing to make others jealous of what we have. Jealousy puts others down; bragging builds us up.'[51]

That's partly why Paul mentions one right after the other; Because he wanted to make sure that those who were *boasting and bragging* understood that they were in *just as much sin* as those as those who were *envious of what they had.*

None of us are exempt from this particular sin, because no one really wants to look bad in front of others.

And since that's the case, we must constantly be *'on our guard'*, and make sure that we don't ever get *carried away* with our *performance*, or our *accomplishments.*

❤ *The Church At Corinth*

It's obvious as we read Paul's first letter to the Corinthians that they were sadly *lacking* this revelation; They were really big spiritual *show-offs*, always looking for *recognition*, and constantly competing for *public attention.*

They sought after the most *prestigious offices* (e.g. Apostle, Prophet, etc.) and the most *glamorous gifts* (miracles & healings) so that they could *flaunt their spirituality* in front of others; that's why Paul said in 1st Corinthians chapter 14 and verse 26…

1 Cor 14:26 What is the outcome then, brethren? When you assemble, each one has a psalm, has a teaching, has a revelation, has a tongue, has an interpretation. Let all things be done for edification ('not as a means to brag on yourselves is what Paul is really saying).
NASB

The Corinthian believers seemed to do their own thing, with

---

51   John F. MacArthur, *The MacArthur New Testament Commentary, 1 Corinthians*, copyright © 1984 by The Moody Bible Institute of Chicago, p.341

total disregard to God, the leadership, and other believers. That's the reason why Paul goes on to say in verses 27 through 33…

1 Cor 14:27 *If anyone speaks in a tongue, it should be by two or at the most three, and each in turn, and let one interpret;*

1 Cor 14:28 *but if there is no interpreter, let him keep silent in the church; and let him speak to himself and to God.*

1 Cor 14:29 *And let two or three prophets speak, and let the others pass judgment.*

1 Cor 14:30 *But if a revelation is made to another who is seated, let the first keep silent.*

1 Cor 14:31 *For you can all prophesy one by one, so that all may learn and all may be exhorted;*

1 Cor 14:32 *and the spirits of prophets are subject to prophets;*

1 Cor 14:33 *for God is not a God of confusion but of peace, as in all the churches of the saints.* [NASB]

C.S. Lewis called bragging *"the utmost evil"*[52], and it's something we must do everything to *keep away from.*

♥ *Jesus Christ – Our Example*

If there was anyone that had everything to boast, and brag about, it was Jesus Christ; But it says about Him, in Philippians chapter 2, verses 6 through 8…

---

52   John F. MacArthur, *The MacArthur New Testament Commentary, 1 Corinthians*, copyright © 1984 by The Moody Bible Institute of Chicago, p.342

Phil 2:6 Who, being in the form of God, thought it not robbery to be equal with God:

Phil 2:7 But made himself of no reputation, and took upon him the form of a servant, and was made in the likeness of men:

Phil 2:8 And being found in fashion as a man, he humbled himself, and became obedient unto death, even the death of the cross. KJV

And the way God responded to this is found in the next three verses which say...

Phil 2:9 Wherefore God also hath highly exalted him, and given him a name which is above every name:

Phil 2:10 That at the name of Jesus every knee should bow, of things in heaven, and things in earth, and things under the earth;

Phil 2:11 And that every tongue should confess that Jesus Christ is Lord, to the glory of God the Father. KJV

There is a great lesson to be learned here: If Jesus could *'make himself of no reputation'*, and *'take on the form of a servant'*, then we, who are to *conform to His image*[53], and *'measure up to the full stature of Christ'*[54], should endeavour to do the same.

Especially since, *in comparison* to His origins and accomplishments, we have *nothing really* to boast about.

Kistemaker says, *"A braggart exhibits pride in himself and his accomplishments. But such bragging is devoid of love to God and to one's fellowman, and is a blatant sin."*[55]

---

53   **Rom 8:29** *For whom He foreknew, He also predestined to be conformed to the image of His Son, that He might be the firstborn among many brethren.* NKJV

54   **Eph 4:13** *until we come to such unity in our faith and knowledge of God's Son that we will be mature and full grown in the Lord, measuring up to the full stature of Christ.* NLT

55   Simon J. Kistemaker, *1 Corinthians*, Baker Books, A Division of Baker Book House Co, Grand Rapids, Michigan 49516, July 2002 p.459

In his commentary, MacArthur adds, "*Only love that comes from Jesus Christ can save us from flaunting our knowledge, our abilities, our gifts, or our accomplishments, real or imagined.*"[56]

To live a life *pleasing to God*, we must *live free from boasting about ourselves*, and *be free to boast about God*, and do as David did, in Psalm 34, verses 1 through 3...

Psa 34:1 *I will bless the LORD at all times; His praise shall continually be in my mouth.*

Psa 34:2 *My soul shall make its boast in the LORD; The humble shall hear of it and be glad.*

Psa 34:3 *Oh, magnify the LORD with me, And let us exalt His name together.* NKJV

---

56   John F. MacArthur, *The MacArthur New Testament Commentary, 1 Corinthians*, copyright © 1984 by The Moody Bible Institute of Chicago, p.342

Chapter 7

LOVE – NOT PROUD OR ARROGANT

❧ Pride & Arrogance

Taking a final look at 1st Corinthians chapter 13 and verse 4, the apostle Paul again writes there…

1 **Cor 13:4** *Love suffers long, and is kind; love does not envy; love does not (brag, boast or) parade itself, is not puffed up,* NKJV

The Greek word for *'puffed up'* (Gk. *'phusioo'*:G5448) means *'to be proud (haughty)*[57] *and arrogant'*[58].

Therefore, in order to understand what *love* is *NOT*, we need to understand what *pride* and *arrogance ARE.*

The Oxford Dictionary[59] defines *'pride'* as *'a high or overbearing opinion of one's worth or importance'.* Jesus teaches about this in Luke chapter 14, verses 8 through 11, where he says…

---

57 *QuickVerse – Strong's Exhaustive Concordance Of The Bible,* The Hebrew and Greek Dictionary is extracted from *Strong's Exhaustive Concordance Of The Bible,* © copyrighted 1980, 1986 and assigned to World Bible Publishers, Inc. All rights reserved.

58 *QuickVerse – NAS Exhaustive Concordance Of The Bible,* © 1981 by the Lockman Foundation, all rights reserved. (*Software Version*)

59 Microsoft® Encarta® 98 Encyclopaedia. The Concise® Oxford Dictionary, 9th Edition. (c) © Oxford University Press. All rights reserved.

Luke 14:8 *"When someone invites you to a wedding feast, do not take the place of honour, for a person more distinguished than you may have been invited.*

Luke 14:9 *If so, the host who invited both of you will come and say to you, 'Give this man your seat.' Then, humiliated, you will have to take the least important place.*

Luke 14:10 *But when you are invited, take the lowest place, so that when your host comes, he will say to you, 'Friend, move up to a better place.' Then you will be honoured in the presence of all your fellow guests.*

Luke 14:11 *For everyone who exalts himself will be humbled, and he who humbles himself will be exalted."* NIV

MacArthur says, *"Arrogance is big-headed; love is big-hearted"*[60].

It is easier to *recognise pride* and *arrogance* in others, than in yourself; It often drives people away, just as bragging and boasting do.

Boastful pride is rebellion against God, because it deliberately takes credit for what God does; That's why the apostle John warns us in 1st John chapter 2 and verse 16...

1 John 2:16 *For all that is in the world, the lust of the flesh and the lust of the eyes and the boastful pride of life, is not from the Father, but is from the world.* NASB

♥ The Sin God Hates

Pride was at the centre of Lucifer's sin against God, and is said to be *"the root and essence of sin"*; That's why Proverbs chapter 6,

---

60   John F. MacArthur, *The MacArthur New Testament Commentary, 1 Corinthians*, copyright © 1984 by The Moody Bible Institute of Chicago, p.343

which lists what God *hates, begins* with *pride,* and starts in verse 16 with...

Prov 6:16 *These six things doth the LORD hate: yea, seven are an abomination unto him:*

Prov 6:17 *A PROUD look, a lying tongue, and hands that shed innocent blood,*

Prov 6:18 *An heart that deviseth wicked imaginations, feet that be swift in running to mischief,*

Prov 6:19 *A false witness that speaketh lies, and he that soweth discord among brethren.*KJV

Prideful arrogance and love are *complete* opposites: they have absolutely *nothing* in common.

In fact, while *love* likes to work *quietly and unannounced,* prideful boasting *looks for an audience*[61].

♥ *Different Forms Of Pride*

Pride can take on many different forms such as *social status, pride of race, academic pride, financial pride, spiritual pride,* and so on.

In Romans chapter 12 and verse 16, the apostle Paul deals with *social status,* and writes...

Rom 12:16 *Live in harmony with one another. Do not be PROUD, but BE WILLING to associate with people of LOW POSITION. Do not be conceited.* NIV

John the Baptist denounces *pride of race* in Luke chapter 3, and says in verse 8...

---

61   *If there was nobody around, who would you boast to?*

Luke 3:8b ...*do not begin to say to yourselves, 'We have Abraham for our father,' for I say to you that God is able from these stones to raise up children to Abraham.* NKJV

Paul dealt with *academic pride* in 1ˢᵗ Corinthians chapter 8 and verse 1, when he said...

1 Cor 8:1b ...*we know that "all of us possess knowledge." Knowledge puffs up, but love builds up.* KJV

When it comes to *pride in the area of finances*, Moses addresses it in Deuteronomy chapter 8, verses 17 and 18, and says...

Deu 8:17 *Do not say to yourself, "My power and the might of my own hand have gotten me this wealth."*

Deu 8:18 *But remember the LORD your God, for it is he who gives you power to get wealth, so that he may confirm his covenant that he swore to your ancestors, as he is doing today.* NRSV

Finally, as to *spiritual pride*, in Luke chapter 18, verses 10 through 14, Jesus shares this parable with us, which says...

Luke 18:10 *"Two men went up to the temple to pray, one a Pharisee and the other a tax collector.*

Luke 18:11 *The Pharisee, standing by himself, was praying thus, 'God, I thank you that I am not like other people: thieves, rogues, adulterers, or even like this tax collector.*

Luke 18:12 *I fast twice a week; I give a tenth of all my income.'*

Luke 18:13 *But the tax collector, standing far off, would not even look up to heaven, but was beating his breast and saying, 'God, be merciful to me, a sinner!'*

Luke 18:14 *I tell you, this man went down to his home justified rather than the other; for all who exalt themselves will be humbled, but all who humble themselves will be exalted.*" NRSV

Kistemaker says that *"Arrogance is inflated selfishness, while love is genuine humility"*[62].

♥ Pride's Opposite: Humility

Humility and *pride* are in total opposition to each other. In 1st Peter chapter 5 and the latter half of verse 5, the apostle Peter (who had some prior experience with this) writes...

1 Pet 5:5b *... all of you must clothe yourselves with humility in your dealings with one another, for "God opposes (Gk. 'to set oneself against'[63]) the proud, but gives grace to the humble."* NRSV

James says the same thing in James chapter 4 and verse 6, and that is...

James 4:6b *..."God opposes the PROUD, but gives GRACE to the HUMBLE."* NRSV

In short, God actually sets Himself *against*, and *opposes* the proud; It is *evil* in His sight. Proverbs chapter 8 and verse 13 says...

Prov 8:13 *To fear the LORD is to hate evil; I hate pride and arrogance, evil behaviour and perverse speech.* NIV

Added to this, Proverbs chapter 13 and verse 10 says...

62 Simon J. Kistemaker, *1 Corinthians*, Baker Books, A Division of Baker Book House Co, Grand Rapids, Michigan 49516, July 2002 p.459

63 *QuickVerse – NAS Exhaustive Concordance Of The Bible*, © 1981 by the Lockman Foundation, all rights reserved. (*Software Version*)

Prov 13:10 Pride only breeds quarrels ([64]contention, debate and strife), but wisdom is found in those who take advice. NIV

Quarrels, debate and strife will eventually lead to shame, disgrace and dishonour, which is why Proverbs chapter 11 and verse 2 says...

Prov 11:2 When pride comes, then comes disgrace ([65]shame and dishonour), but with humility comes wisdom. NIV

What's more, in Proverbs chapter 29 and verse 23, it also promises...

Prov 29:23 A person's pride will bring humiliation, but one who is lowly in spirit will obtain honour. NRSV

It's because of all these negative qualities that are associated with pride and arrogance that Proverbs chapter 16 and verse 18 tells us...

Prov 16:18 Pride goes before destruction, and a haughty spirit before a fall. NRSV

In short, because of their *attitude* and *behaviour*, this verse tells us that proud people are headed for *destruction*, and will ultimately *fall*.

But as *harmful* and *damaging* as *pride* is, the Scriptures show *humility* to have the *exact, opposite effect*.

---

64   Gk. '*Quarrels*' *QuickVerse – Strong's Exhaustive Concordance Of The Bible*, The Hebrew and Greek Dictionary is extracted from *Strong's Exhaustive Concordance Of The Bible*, © copyrighted 1980, 1986 and assigned to World Bible Publishers, Inc. All rights reserved.

65   Gk. '*Shame, dishonour*' *QuickVerse – Strong's Exhaustive Concordance Of The Bible*, The Hebrew and Greek Dictionary is extracted from *Strong's Exhaustive Concordance Of The Bible*, © copyrighted 1980, 1986 and assigned to World Bible Publishers, Inc. All rights reserved.

♥ Humble Yourself Before God

The Pictorial Bible Dictionary defines *humility* as *'freedom from pride'*[66].

Jesus said in Matthew chapter 23 and verse 12...

Mat 23:12 *All who exalt themselves will be humbled, and all who humble themselves will be exalted.* NRSV

This was exactly what Jesus Himself did. And as a result, following His humiliating death on the cross, the apostle Paul recorded in Philippians chapter 2, verses 8 through 11...

Phil 2:8 *And being found in appearance as a man, HE HUMBLED HIMSELF by becoming obedient to the point of death, even death on a cross.*

Phil 2:9 *Therefore also GOD HIGHLY EXALTED HIM, and bestowed on Him the name which is above every name,*

Phil 2:10 *that at the name of Jesus every knee should bow, of those who are in heaven, and on earth, and under the earth,*

Phil 2:11 *and that every tongue should confess that Jesus Christ is Lord, to the glory of God the Father.* NASB

Everything that *pride* lusts after has *already* been assigned to *the humble*: Peter learned this valuable lesson and wrote in 1st Peter chapter 5, verses 6 and 7...

1 Pet 5:6 *Humble yourselves therefore under the mighty hand of God, that He may exalt you in due time:*

1 Pet 5:7 *Casting all your care upon Him; for He careth for you.* KJV

---

66   Pictorial Bible Dictionary, *The Zondervan Pictorial Bible Dictionary*, Copyright © 1963, 1964, 1967 by Zondervan Publishing House, Grand Rapids, Michigan.

Added to this, James writes in James chapter 4, verses 6 and 7...

James 4:6b ..."*God opposes the proud, but gives grace to the humble.*"

James 4:7 *Submit yourselves therefore to God. Resist the devil, and he will flee from you.*NRSV

Even your authority is based on your *humility* and *submission* to God. It's not something that just happens automatically. We have to make a choice to do it, or as the apostle Paul puts it in Colossians chapter 3 and verse 12...

Col 3:12 *As God's chosen ones, holy and beloved, clothe yourselves with (or choose to 'put on') compassion, kindness, humility, meekness, and patience.* NRSV

In fact, our very 'calling' depends on it according to Ephesians chapter 4, verses 1 through 3, where the apostle Paul writes...

Eph 4:1 *I therefore, the prisoner in the Lord, beg you to lead a life worthy of the calling to which you have been called,*

Eph 4:2 *with all humility and gentleness, with patience, bearing with one another in love,*

Eph 4:3 *making every effort to maintain the unity of the Spirit in the bond of peace.* NRSV

Before we move, I'd like to, very quickly, deal with one other trait that works very closely with *humility*, and that's *meekness*, defined as 'controlled power'.

♥ Blessed Are The Meek

Like *humility*, *meekness* is pride's *other* opposite.

In fact, if you are ever going to learn anything at all, you have to let go of pride and become meek and teachable. The apostle James writes in James chapter 1 and verse 21…

James 1:21 *Wherefore lay apart all filthiness and superfluity of naughtiness, and receive with meekness (humility* [NIV]*) the engrafted word, which is able to save your souls.* [KJV]

As a result of the receptivity of the meek – their heart and hunger for knowledge – Jesus says in Matthew chapter 5 and verse 5…

Mat 5:5 *Blessed are the meek: for they shall inherit the earth.* [KJV]

Notice again that, *everything* the *proud* desires to have, 'the meek' will receive by, and through, *inheritance.*

Furthermore, the apostle James goes as far as to say that *meek, gentle* and *humble* people are considered wise according to James chapter 3 and verse 13, which reads…

James 3:13 *Who is wise and understanding among you? Show by your good life that your works are done with gentleness (meekness* [NKJV]*, humility* [NIV]*) born of wisdom.* [NRSV]

This is the wisdom that is required to share the Gospel according to 1st Peter chapter 3, verses 15 and 16, where the apostle Peter says…

1 Pet 3:15 *But in your hearts set apart Christ as Lord. Always be prepared to give an answer to everyone who asks you to give the reason for the hope that you have. But do this with gentleness (meekness* [NKJV]*) and respect,*

1 Pet 3:16 *keeping a clear conscience, so that those who speak maliciously against your good behaviour in Christ may be ashamed of their slander.* [NIV]

The mistake that many Christians make is that, instead of doing what Peter said here, and treating those that *believe differently* with *gentleness, meekness* and *respect*, they arrogantly attack them with the Gospel, and wonder why these people don't get saved.

If you *value people*, they will *value you* and *value what you say*; If you don't, they won't.

Even the apostle Paul had the same revelation that Peter had, and wrote in 2ⁿᵈ Timothy chapter 2, verses 24 and 25...

2 Tim 2:24 *And the Lord's servant must not be quarrelsome but kindly to everyone, an apt teacher, patient,*

2 Tim 2:25 *correcting opponents with gentleness.* ᴺᴿˢⱽ *(meekness* ᴷᴶⱽ, *and humility* ᴺᴷᴶⱽ*)*

Let me conclude this quality with a true story[67].

William Carey, who has come to be known as 'the father of modern missions', was a brilliant linguist, and was responsible for translating parts of the Bible into more than 34 different languages and dialects!

He was raised in a simple home in England, and as a young man, worked as a cobbler.

In India he often was ridiculed for his "low" birth and former occupation.

At a dinner party one evening, a snob said, "I understand, Mister Carey, that you once worked as a shoemaker".

"Oh no, your lordship", Carey replied, "I was not a shoemaker, only a shoe repairman."

Dale Burke[68] *writes...*

The humble can wait patiently, while **the arrogant** *wants it now!*

The humble demonstrate kindness, while **the arrogant** *don't even notice the need.*

---

67   John F. MacArthur, *The MacArthur New Testament Commentary, 1 Corinthians*, copyright © 1984 by The Moody Bible Institute of Chicago, p.343

68   H. Dale Burke, *A Love That Never Fails: 1 Corinthians 13*, © 1999 by H. Dale Burke and Jac La Tour, Moody Press, Chicago. p.56

The humble are content, not jealous or envious, while **the arrogant** feel they deserve more.

The humble honours and esteems the other, while **the arrogant** brags on himself.

The humble does not act unbecomingly, while **the arrogant's** manners are rude.

The humble shows a servant spirit, while **the arrogant** demands to be served.

The humble are not easily provoked, while **the arrogant** are quick to take offence.

The humble quickly forgive a wrong suffered, while **the arrogant** can't resist until they 'even the score'.

Chapter 8

LOVE IS NOT RUDE

❧ Behaviour Contrary To Love

We now come to verse 5, of 1ˢᵗ Corinthians chapter 13, and encounter the *fourth* of eight qualities of what '*love is not*', and that is it...

1 Cor 13:5a *Does not behave rudely (or 'unbecomingly'* ᴺᴬˢᴮ*),...* ᴺᴷᴶⱽ mod.

Kistemaker[69] says, "*Paul has in mind unbecoming, improper [indecent], and inappropriate behaviour in any situation.*"

He continues[70], "*Decent behaviour does not stop with words and attitude. It also pertains to one's apparel and appearance. Proper dress and a groomed look commend a person who desires to please others, for love extends to all aspects of one's demeanour.*"

The apostle Paul says in Romans chapter 13 and verse 13, from the New Living Translation...

69   Simon J. Kistemaker, *1 Corinthians*, Baker Books, A Division of Baker Book House Co, Grand Rapids, Michigan 49516, July 2002 p.459

70   Simon J. Kistemaker, *1 Corinthians*, Baker Books, A Division of Baker Book House Co, Grand Rapids, Michigan 49516, July 2002 p.460

Rom 13:13a *We should be decent and true in everything we do (or 'Let us behave decently' says the NIV), so that everyone can approve of our behaviour.* ^{NLT}

John MacArthur[71] *says, "the principle here has to do with poor manners; with acting rudely. It is not as serious a fault as bragging or arrogance, but it stems from the same lovelessness;"*

"*Rude people* don't care enough for those around them to act politely; They are often *crude, overbearing* and *careless*."

The Corinthian Christians seemed to excel in this type of behaviour. And as a result, the apostle Paul says to them in 1st Corinthians chapter 11, verses 20 through 22...

1 Cor 11:20 *When you come together, it is not really to eat the Lord's supper.*

1 Cor 11:21 *For when the time comes to eat, each of you goes ahead with your own supper, and one goes hungry and another becomes drunk.*

1 Cor 11:22 *What! Do you not have homes to eat and drink in? Or do you show contempt for the church of God and humiliate those who have nothing? What should I say to you? Should I commend you? In this matter I do not commend you!* ^{NRSV}

And it didn't stop there. As you know, in 1st Corinthians chapter 14, Paul goes on to reprimand them about their behaviour during their worship services, with each one trying to outdo the other in speaking in tongues, prophecy, and so on.

Dale Burke[72] *says that the Greek root ('aschemoneo':G807) that's translated 'rude' or 'unbecomingly'* literally means "*without shape*"

---

71 John F. MacArthur, *The MacArthur New Testament Commentary, 1 Corinthians*, copyright © 1984 by The Moody Bible Institute of Chicago, p.343

72 H. Dale Burke, *A Love That Never Fails: 1 Corinthians 13*, © 1999 by H. Dale Burke and Jac La Tour, Moody Press, Chicago. p.64

and is always used in the New Testament to refer to *behaviour* that is "*out of shape*" or "*out of bounds*".

♥ Godly Behaviour

Its *opposite form* is *prominence*, used to describe those who have *good taste, class, style* and *reputation* [73] like those who became believers in Acts 17:12, and Joseph of Arimathea, mentioned in Mark chapter 15 and verse 43, who requested the body of Jesus and got it, because it says that he was "*a prominent, honoured member of council.*"[74]

In other words, *a part of walking in love* is to have *good taste, class, style* and *reputation*; And those that don't, or '*behave rudely*' are actually *out of God's will*.

Simple things such as *not* saying '*please*', '*thank you*', '*excuse me*', '*sorry*', '*what can I do to help you*', or even a simple '*you first*', puts you in this category of being *rude* and *unbecoming*.

In 2ⁿᵈ Thessalonians chapter 3, verses 6 through 9, the apostle Paul says...

2 Th 3:6 In the name of the Lord Jesus Christ, we command you, brothers, to keep away from every brother who is idle and does not live according to the teaching you received from us.

2 Th 3:7 For you yourselves know how you ought to follow our example. We were not idle (or 'We did not act in an undisciplined manner' [NASB]*) when we were with you (meaning that he was courteous, considerate and well-mannered at all times),*

---

73   H. Dale Burke, *A Love That Never Fails: 1 Corinthians 13*, © 1999 by H. Dale Burke and Jac La Tour, Moody Press, Chicago. p.64

74   **Mark 15:43** NIV - *Joseph of Arimathea, a prominent member of the Council...*; NLT - *an honoured member of the high council,...*

2 Th 3:8 *nor did we eat anyone's food without paying for it (here's an example of Paul being courteous and well-mannered; It goes on to say...). On the contrary, we worked night and day, labouring and toiling so that we would not be a burden to any of you (here's Paul being considerate of others).*

2 Th 3:9 *We did this, not because we do not have the right to such help, but in order to make ourselves a model for you to follow.* ^{NIV}

Love is *deeply concerned* about the *feelings* of others. And people know when you genuinely care about them. Sometimes that's all it takes to open the door to share the Gospel with them.

Let's make sure that our manners, like that of the Corinthian church (who were self-centred and offensive), don't stop people from coming into the kingdom of God, because that would be tragic; That's why Paul concludes in 1st Corinthians 14:40 with...

1 Cor 14:40 *Let all things be done decently and in order.* ^{KJV}

The best way to *let* people know that you love them, is to do as the apostle Paul did in 2nd Thessalonians 3 (vs.6-9), and *show* them you love them, in both *word* and *deed*, and especially by your *good manners*, and your *godly behaviour*.

Chapter 9

LOVE – NOT SELFISH OR SELF-CENTRED

❧ Love Does Not Seek It's Own

Returning to 1ˢᵗ Corinthians 13 and verse 5, we now come to the *fifth* of eight qualities that Paul says '*love is not*'; Specifically, that love…

1 Cor 13:5b *…does not seek its own,…* ᴷᴶⱽ

Burke says, *A more literal rendering might be "Love does not seek to further its own profit or advantage."*

In other words, *love is not selfish or self-centred.* Never will anyone say of it, as was said on a certain individual's tombstone, in a small English village…

> "Here lies a miser who lived for himself,
>   and cared for nothing but gathering wealth.
> "Now where he is, or how he fares,
>   nobody knows and nobody cares."

Love would have a different inscription, one like that found on a plain tombstone in the court-yard at St. Paul's, in London, that reads...

"Sacred to the memory of General Charles George Gordon,
who at all times and everywhere gave his strength to the weak,
his substance to the poor, his sympathy to the suffering, his
heart to God."

R. C. H. Lenski, a well-known Bible commentator once said, *"Cure Selfishness and you have just re-planted the garden of Eden."*[75]

♥ Putting Others First

At the fall of man, *'self'* replaced God; And it took the cross of Jesus Christ to restore what was lost. But, it *has* been restored, and that's why the apostle Paul now encourages us in 1ˢᵗ Corinthians chapter 10 and verse 24...

1 Cor 10:24 *Don't think only of your own good. Think of other Christians and what is best for them.* ᴺᴸᵀ

In other words, Paul says, make the good of others one of your primary goals; And he goes on further to say in verse 33...

1 Cor 10:33 *That is the plan I follow, too. I try to please everyone in everything I do. I don't just do what I like or what is best for me, but what is best for them so they may be saved.*ᴺᴸᵀ

What we see from these verses is that, God's love, which is a *genuine, caring love*, is not preoccupied with its own interests, but the interest of others to the point that people feel *valued* and *appreciated*, and *receptive* to the Gospel, and ultimately, *salvation*.

---

75   Taken from John F. MacArthur, *The MacArthur New Testament Commentary, 1 Corinthians,* copyright © 1984 by The Moody Bible Institute of Chicago, p.344-345

In Philippians chapter 2, verses 3 and 4, the apostle Paul says...

Phil 2:3 *Do nothing from selfish ambition or conceit, but in humility regard others as better than yourselves.*

Phil 2:4 *Let each of you look NOT to your own interests, but to the interests of others.* ^{NRSV}

That's the positive aspect of *'love does not seek its own',* and is precisely what love is: *putting others interests ahead of its own.*

♥ Forget About Yourself

In fact, that's one of the most healing things you can do: Forget about yourself.

A lot of the problems we face in the world today come from *selfishness* and *self-centredness*; James was well aware of this and wrote in James chapter 4, verses 1 through 3...

James 4:1 *From whence come wars and fightings among you? come they not hence, even of your lusts that war in your members?*

James 4:2 *Ye lust, and have not: ye kill, and desire to have, and cannot obtain: ye fight and war, yet ye have not, because ye ask not.*

James 4:3 *Ye ask, and receive not, because ye ask amiss, that ye may consume it upon your lusts.* ^{KJV}

James shows us in these verses the lengths people are willing to go to, to get what they want; And most don't care who they hurt and injure to get what they want.

In direct contrast to this is the God-kind of love which will go out of its way to help and bless others, regardless of the obstacles that come its way.

I'd like to conclude this particular quality with the following, taken from John MacArthur's commentary on 1st Corinthians[76]:

The story is told of a chauffeur, who drove up to a cemetery and asked the minister, who served as caretaker, to come to the car, because his employer was too ill to walk.

Waiting in the car was a frail old lady with sunken eyes that showed years of hurt and anguish.

She introduced herself and said she had been sending five dollars to the cemetery for the past several years to be used for flowers for her husband's grave.

"I have come in person today," she said, "because the doctors have given me only a few weeks to live and I wanted to see the grave for one last time."

The minister replied, "You know, I'm sorry that you've been sending money for those flowers."

Taken back, she said, "What do you mean?"

"Well, I happen to be a part of a visiting society that visits patients in hospitals and mental institutions.

"They dearly love flowers.

"They can see them and smell them.

"Flowers are therapy for them, because they are living people."

Saying nothing, she motioned the chauffeur to leave.

Some months later, the minister was surprised to see the same car drive up, but with the woman herself at the wheel.

She said, "At first I resented what you said to me that day when I came here for a last visit.

"But as I thought about it, I decided you were right.

"Now I personally take flowers to the hospitals.

"It DOES make the patients happy and it makes me happy, too.

"The doctors can't figure out what made me well, but I know, I now I have someone else to live for."

---

76   John F. MacArthur, *The MacArthur New Testament Commentary, 1 Corinthians*, copyright © 1984 by The Moody Bible Institute of Chicago, p.345

Jesus put it best, when He said in Matthew chapter 20 and verse 28…

Mat 20:28b *…the Son of Man did not come to be served, but to serve, and to give His life a ransom for many."* NASB

This is the commission we've been given. And it is up to us to fulfil it.

We only have one chance to do it, and it only lasts as long as we are here on this earth.

Once we are in Heaven, there'll be no adding to it, just the enjoyment of the fruits of our labour (or lack thereof).

Chapter 10

LOVE IS NOT PROVOKED EASILY

❧ Love – Not Irritated, Upset Or Angry

Returning again to 1st Corinthians 13 and verse 5, we now come to the *sixth* of eight qualities that Paul says *'love is not'*; And this time, it's love is…

1 Cor 13:5c …*not provoked,*… ᴷᴶⱽ

The Greek word (Gk. *'paroxuno'*:G3947) translated *"provoked"* means *"to arouse to anger"* and originates from an English word (*paroxysm*) that conveys *"a convulsion or sudden outburst of emotion or action."*[77]

Therefore, *'to be provoked'* means to be *irritated, upset* and *angry*: All of which *love guards against.*

♥ *Righteous Anger*

Before we go any further, we must understand that the Bible *never* tells us that we *shouldn't* feel angry; However, it does *insist* that we

---

77   John F. MacArthur, *The MacArthur New Testament Commentary, 1 Corinthians*, copyright © 1984 by The Moody Bible Institute of Chicago, p.345

become *angry* about the *right* things, and that we *handle* our anger *correctly.*

This is *true* spiritual warfare: *Refusing* to *allow* yourself to be *provoked* or *angered* over *personal* attacks, while remaining open to *righteous anger*, and being *wise* enough to *know* the difference.

Paul talks about righteous anger in Ephesians chapter 4 and verse 26, when he writes…

Eph 4:26 Be ye angry, and sin not: let not the sun go down upon your wrath: KJV

Righteous anger passionately *opposes* evil, as was the case with Jesus in Matthew chapter 21, where it says, in verses 11 through 13…

Mat 21:11 The crowds were saying, "This is the prophet Jesus from Nazareth in Galilee."

Mat 21:12 Then Jesus entered the temple and drove out all who were selling and buying in the temple, and he overturned the tables of the money changers and the seats of those who sold doves.

Mat 21:13 He said to them, "It is written, 'My house shall be called a house of prayer'; but you are making it a den of robbers." NRSV

The reason for the Lord's *anger* was because the money changers had set up their booths and were conducting business on a regular basis in the area of the temple referred to as '*The Court of the Gentiles*', which was meant to be *reserved* for Gentile worship.

And with all the business activity going on, the crowds would build, leaving little or no room for Gentiles to come and worship God in the temple.

Added to this was all the dishonesty going on: First, there were the money-changers who held the only currency accepted by the merchants, in the form of 'temple coins', and who would constantly *cheat* and *steal* from the Gentiles, by way of *unfair* exchange rates.

Second, there were the merchants, who sold the sacrifices to people who found it difficult to bring their own sacrifices over long distances and *over-charged* them for these animals, thereby robbing them *twice-over* in a single day.

Everyone who lived there, including Jesus, knew *exactly* what was going on, and for the first time *ever*, somebody actually stood up, *got angry* and *put a stop* to what was going on in the temple, all '*in the Name of God*'.

❤ *Unrighteous Anger*

In direct contrast to this *righteous anger*, is *selfish anger* and *rage*, which Psalm 37 and verse 8 talks about, and says…

*Psa 37:8 Stop your anger! Turn from your rage! Do not envy others-- it only leads to harm.*NLT

The husband or wife that constantly yells at their spouse, while at the same time tells them they love them aren't walking in the God-kind of love;

And neither are the parents of children that tell their kids how much they love them, but never stop yelling at them.

Temper bombs, even though they don't last long can have *long lasting effects* on people, and must be kept under control, and over-come in time, if you don't want to be considered a fool; Because that's what Ecclesiastes chapter 7 and verse 9 means, when it says…

Eccl 7:9 Don't be quick-tempered, for anger is the friend of fools. NLT

Only *foolish people* entertain, and indulge in, *selfish anger*; The wise know to stay well away from it, because it leads to *harm*.

♥ *Wisdom To Control Your Anger*

Proverbs chapter 16 and verse 32 says…

Prov 16:32 *Better a patient man than a warrior, a man who controls his temper than one who takes a city.* ^{NIV}

In short, God esteems a *patient person*, who is in *control* of his anger, as being far greater than *a warrior* who is able to conquer *a city*, all on his own.

Jesus *demonstrated* this kind of *strength* when he was physically *injured*, and grossly *mistreated* on the way to the cross, to suffer for *our* sins, setting an example for us all to follow, as Peter did, and why he wrote, in 1st Peter chapter 2,verses 21 through 24…

1 Pet 2:21 *For to this YOU have been called, because Christ also suffered for you, leaving you an example, so that you should follow in his steps.*

1 Pet 2:22 *"He committed no sin, and no deceit was found in his mouth."*

1 Pet 2:23 *When he was abused, he did not return abuse; when he suffered, he did not threaten; but he entrusted himself to the one who judges justly.*

1 Pet 2:24 *He himself bore our sins in his body on the cross, so that, free from sins, we might live for righteousness; by his wounds you have been healed.* ^{NRSV}

Remember, this suffering was endured for *our* benefit, not because He did anything wrong, but because of *our* sin and transgression against God.

That's when it's hardest to *not* get *angry* and *upset*; When you are *falsely accused* and being punished for *someone else's* crime.

It is in times like these that we must remember that we are, in fact, *more* than conquerors[78] and learn to face these adversities with *patience, calmness* and *confidence,* remembering that *God will always have the final say* according to Romans 12:19 which states…

Rom 12:19 *Dear friends, never avenge yourselves. Leave that to God. For it is written, "I will take vengeance; I will repay those who deserve it," says the Lord.* NLT

So, once again, returning to 1st Corinthians 13:5, it says that *God's love* makes the decision *not* to be provoked, and that must become our decision as well if we are ever going to live a life that is pleasing to God.

It is a decision that will take *time* for us to *mature* in, but be rest assured, with God's help, it *will* happen.

Chapter 11

LOVE DOES NOT REJOICE IN INIQUITY

❧ Love Does No Wrong

Returning again to 1st Corinthians 13, this time we'll begin in verse 6 (since we covered forgiveness in Part 1), and we now come to the *eighth* and final quality that Paul says *'love is not'*, and that is, love...

1 Cor 13:6a *does not rejoice in iniquity...* NKJV

Other translations translate *'iniquity'* as *'evil* NIV, *wrongdoing* NRSV, *unrighteousness* NASB *and injustice* NLT*.'*

Therefore, to *'rejoice in iniquity'* means *'to enjoy sin in its various forms'*; And this says that *love* not only doesn't take satisfaction from *evil*, *wrongdoing*, *unrighteousness* and *injustice*, but it doesn't *brag* about it either.[79]

In other words, it doesn't go around parading its *'goodness.'*

In his commentary on 1st Corinthians, *John F. MacArthur* says,

---

79   Some examples of this include *stealing* from others and bragging about it; Or, having *intimate relations* with someone and telling all your friends about it; Or, *deceiving* someone, and patting yourself on the back over it, and so on.

"Among the most popular magazines, book and TV programs are those that glorify sin, that literally rejoice in unrighteousness."[80]

He adds, "Sometimes rejoicing in unrighteousness takes the form of hoping someone will make a mistake or fall into sin."[81]

It is essential that we understand that the sin of others, believers *and* unbelievers, actually *hurts* and *grieves* our Heavenly Father.

And if we love God with *all our heart, soul* and *mind*[82], then what affects Him should affect us, and we should have the same attitude that David had in Psalm 69 and verse 9, and that is…

Psa 69:9b … *the insults of those who insult You have fallen on me.*
NRSV

Jesus was no different. The writer of Hebrews says, in Hebrews chapter 1 and verse 9…

Heb 1:9 *You have loved RIGHTEOUSNESS and hated WICK-EDNESS; therefore God, your God, has anointed you with the oil of gladness beyond your companions."* NRSV

♥ *Rejoicing Over Another's Downfall*

One way to *rejoice in sin* is to *gloat over the shortcomings of others*, commonly referred to as 'gossip'.

And even though so many Christians treat this *sin* lightly, it is still *evil*; And just for the record, *gossip* that is *true*, is *still* gossip.

It's the way that *satan's victories* in peoples lives are *passed on*

---

80   John F. MacArthur, *The MacArthur New Testament Commentary, 1 Corinthians*, copyright © 1984 by The Moody Bible Institute of Chicago, p.349

81   John F. MacArthur, *The MacArthur New Testament Commentary, 1 Corinthians*, copyright © 1984 by The Moody Bible Institute of Chicago, p.350

82   **Mat 22:37-38** *Jesus said unto him, Thou shalt love the Lord thy God with all thy heart, and with all thy soul, and with all thy mind. This is the first and great commandment.* KJV

from one person to the next, and advertised, which is what makes it so *destructive*, and why it *grieves* God so much.

The sad thing is, this sin would do *very little harm* if it did not have so many *willing* participants.

We must learn to distinguish between 'the sinner' and 'the sin'; When we do, we will better understand what we are to *expose*, and what we are to *protect*.

The apostle Paul says in Ephesians chapter 4 and verse 29...

Eph 4:29 Do not let any unwholesome talk (including 'gossip' that is true) come out of your mouths, but only what is helpful for building others up according to their needs, that it may benefit those who listen. NIV

♥ *Hurting People With The Truth*

Dale Burke says[83]*, "Honesty is not a license to kill with our words. It's a permit to build, not to destroy."*

It is possible to *expose sin* and *protect the dignity of the sinner*, all at the same time; But it takes *wisdom* and *the leading of the Spirit* to do it.

Those without either will go around hurting people '*in the Name of God'*, thinking that they are doing God, and the Body of Christ a great service, when, in fact, all they are doing is helping the devil *defeat*, and *destroy* the church, one person at a time.

In his commentary, *MacArthur* shares the following[84]: *A person is never helped by spreading the news of his sin.* He continues, *Granville Walker* said...

There are times when silence is 'yellow', times when we ought to

---

83   H. Dale Burke, *A Love That Never Fails: 1 Corinthians 13*, © 1999 by H. Dale Burke and Jac La Tour, Moody Press, Chicago. p.129

84   John F. MacArthur, *The MacArthur New Testament Commentary, 1 Corinthians*, copyright © 1984 by The Moody Bible Institute of Chicago, p.350

stand on our feet and, regardless of the consequences, challenge the gross evils of the time, times when not to do so is the most blatant form of cowardice.

But there are other times when silence is 'golden', when to tell the truth is to make many hearts bleed needlessly and when nothing is accomplished and everything is hurt by a loose tongue.

Here again we see the delicate balance between *love* and *light*; When to *expose evil*, and when to *hold our tongues*.

It is yet another (*more subtle*) way that 'love does not rejoice in iniquity': It does not rejoice in judging people *in* truth *without* grace. Because that, quite simply, is sin.

That's why John chapter 1 and verse 14 says of Jesus…

John 1:14 *And the Word became flesh, and dwelt among us, and we beheld His glory, glory as of the only begotten from the Father, full of grace and truth.* NKJV

Notice that Jesus was not only full of 'truth', but 'grace'. Furthermore, I want you to notice that grace was first, then truth. And that's the way it must always be. Never the other way around.

Chapter 12

LOVE REJOICES IN THE TRUTH

❧ Love's Two-Fold 'Truth'

Returning to 1st Corinthians 13 and the latter half of verse 6, we now come to the *third* of seven qualities that Paul says *'love is'* (the first two being patience and kindness that we dealt with previously), and that is, love…

1 **Cor 13:6b** … *rejoices in the truth (Gk.'aletheia':G225);* NKJV

The *'truth'* that is referred to here is not only *'factual truth'*, but *'The Truth of God's Word'* that Jesus says He is, in John chapter 14 and verse 6 where it is written…

John 14:6 *Jesus said to him, I am the way, the truth (Gk.'aletheia': G225), and the life. No one comes to the Father except through Me.* NKJV

♥ *Factual Truth*

Let's begin with *'factual truth'*, meaning that, "love rejoices in *honesty, sincerity* and *integrity*"; All of which we desperately *need*, both in the Body of Christ and the world today.

In Jeremiah chapter 5 and verse 1, it says...

Jer 5:1 *"Go up and down the streets of Jerusalem, look around and consider, search through her squares. If you can find but one person who DEALS HONESTLY and SEEKS THE TRUTH, I will forgive this city.* ^{NIV}

The future of this *entire city* was dependent on a *single person* being *honest,* and *doing the right thing.*

So much of the time, *simple honesty and sincerity is all* God is looking for. It is what opens the door to *His grace and mercy,* and allows His *divine favour* to work unhindered.

And if we've committed any sins, there's always 1st John 1:9[85] that promises God's immediate *forgiveness* and *cleansing* from *all unrighteousness.*

However, if we are *dishonest* and try to *hide* the truth in the interest of *self-preservation,* then there's not a lot God can do to help us.

John chapter 1 and verse 17 tells us...

John 1:17 *For the law was given through Moses, but grace and truth came through Jesus Christ.* ^{NKJV}

Since *grace and truth* have already *come* through Jesus Christ, and are now available to us, it is time we *learned* how to operate in them, and bless others through them.

To help me with this, God gave me this simple rule to live by: Be *completely honest and truthful* when it comes to *telling on yourself* (so-to-speak), and *full of mercy and grace* when it comes to *telling on others.*

---

85   *1 John 1:9 If we confess our sins, He is faithful and just to forgive us our sins and to cleanse us from all unrighteousness.* ^{NKJV}

♥ God's Word As Truth

There is another area of 'truth' that needs to be dealt with, which is that of the 'the Truth of God's Word'[86]; Jesus said in John chapter 17 and verse 17...

John 17:17 Sanctify them through thy truth: thy word is truth. KJV

So, here Jesus identifies 'the Word of God' as 'Truth'; And just so we don't misunderstand or misinterpret it, in John chapter 16 and verse 13, He says...

John 16:13a Howbeit when he, THE SPIRIT OF TRUTH, is come, he will guide you into all TRUTH: KJV

So, not only do we have 'The Truth of God's Word', but we also have been given 'The Spirit of Truth' to *help us*, and *guide us* into 'all Truth'.

Now, when it comes to *truth*, there are *two types* that stand in direct opposition to each other; They are *spiritual truth* and *natural truth*: Spiritual truth is 'the Truth' of God's Word and natural truth is best described as *what's true* for the moment.

It is in relation to this that the apostle Paul writes in 2nd Corinthians chapter 4 and verse 18...

2 Cor 4:18 While we look not at the things which are seen, but at the things which are not seen: for the things which are seen are temporal; but the things which are not seen are eternal. KJV

In other words, 'The Truth' will always *overcome* and *change* what is 'currently *true*' in our lives, as long as we do what Paul says in 2nd Corinthians 5:7, and that is to...

2 Cor 5:7b ...walk by faith, not by sight. NKJV

---

86 *John 17:17 Sanctify them through thy truth: thy word is truth.* KJV

As we *do* walk *by faith*, we must make sure to always give people something to *agree* with, such as "*I believe I'm healed according to* 1ˢᵗ *Peter* 2:24".

What we must avoid doing is saying things like, "*I'm fine*" when everybody can see that you are not. If you do, you will end up *isolating* yourself, and being *alone* in your faith.

And even in the case of *unbelievers*, you can always say, "*I know it looks bad, but I am on the road to recovery*"; By doing that, it gives them something that even *they* can *agree* with.

Now, since we understand '*The Truth*' to mean *The Word of God*, then one other aspect of '*love rejoicing in the Truth*' would mean that it directly opposes *false doctrines*.

That means, *genuine, godly love* doesn't just stand by and allow people to be *deceived* by *false religions* and *false ideas*, but it is *deeply concerned* about people knowing the truth, and having that truth, set them free.

Jesus said in John chapter 8 and verse 32...

John 8:32 "*And you shall know the truth, and the truth shall make you free.*"ᴺᴷᴶⱽ

Notice two things here: First, it is '*the truth*' and not religious doctrines that is going to set you free; Second, and probably of greater importance, is the fact that, it is only '*the truth*' you *know*, that is going to *save* you, and *free* you.

♥ *Speaking The Truth In Love*

Now, as to *how* we are to communicate this truth is brought out in Ephesians chapter 4, verses 14 and 15, where the apostle Paul writes...

Eph 4:14 *that we should no longer be children, tossed to and fro and carried about with every wind of doctrine, by the trickery of men, in the cunning craftiness of deceitful plotting,*

Eph 4:15 *but, speaking the truth in love, may grow up in all things into Him who is the head; Christ;* NKJV

In other words, whether we are communicating 'factual truth', or 'the truth of the Gospel', we are to *always* do it *in love*; That's what will cause people to *grow up* in *all things*, especially 'into *Him Who is the Head, even Christ'.*

Chapter 13

LOVE BEARS ALL THINGS

❧ Love's Protective Nature

Back in 1ˢᵗ Corinthians 13, we now come to verse 7, where Paul lists the last four qualities of *love*, all of which are *positive*, beginning with...

1 Cor 13:7a *[Love] Bears all things ...* ᴺᴷᴶⱽ

Firstly, the '*all things*' mentioned in each of the qualities to follow are '*all things acceptable to God*' and '*tolerated by God*';

In no way does love *bear, believe, hope* or *endure* lies, false teaching, or anything else that is not of God.

Second, in the Greek, the word '*bear*' (Gk. '*stego*':G4722) actually means '*to cover, support and therefore, protect*'[87].

MacArthur writes,"Love bears all things by protecting others from exposure, ridicule, or harm. ... Even when a sin is certain, love tries to correct it with the least possible hurt and harm to the guilty person. Love never protects sin, but is anxious to protect the sinner."[88]

---

87   John F. MacArthur, *The MacArthur New Testament Commentary, 1 Corinthians,* copyright © 1984 by The Moody Bible Institute of Chicago, p.352

88   John F. MacArthur, *The MacArthur New Testament Commentary, 1 Corinthians,* copyright © 1984 by The Moody Bible Institute of Chicago, p.352

Proverbs chapter 10 and verse 12 has something very interesting to say about this, and that is…

Prov 10:12 Hatred stirs up dissension (& strife [KJV]*), but love covers over all wrongs* [NIV] *(sins* [NKJV]*, transgressions* [NASB]*, and/or offences* [NLT]*).*

In other words, those that aren't developed in *God's love* magnify sin and *stir up* all kinds of *strife* and *dissension*, usually by word of mouth, which is why the apostle James says in James chapter 3, verses 8 through 10…

James 3:8 but no one can tame the tongue. It is an uncontrollable evil, full of deadly poison.

James 3:9 Sometimes it praises our Lord and Father, and sometimes it breaks out into curses against those who have been made in the image of God.

James 3:10 And so blessing and cursing come pouring out of the same mouth. Surely, my brothers and sisters, this is NOT right! [NLT]

Love, on the other hand, according to Proverbs 10:12, *covers up* and *conceals* peoples *sins* and *transgressions*, giving them time to *deal* with them and *overcome* them in their lives.

Kistemaker says that, "*Love is the virtue 'that throws a cloak of silence over what is displeasing in another person*"[89].

In Proverbs chapter 17 and verse 9, it says…

Prov 17:9 He who COVERS OVER an offense promotes LOVE, but whoever repeats the matter separates close friends. [NIV]

In other words, even the closest of friends can be torn apart by the things people say.

---

89 Simon J. Kistemaker, *1 Corinthians*, Baker Books, A Division of Baker Book House Co, Grand Rapids, Michigan 49516, July 2002 p.461

However, love doesn't behave this way; It will go as far as to actually form *a hedge of protection* around the person in an effort to keep them from getting unnecessarily hurt and injured along the way – just another way love *'covers all things'.*

You can actually *measure your love* for a person by *how quickly* you *cover up their faults*: We do this constantly with our children whenever they *make a mistake* or *do something wrong*; It's time we did the same for others.

The apostle Peter writes, in 1st Peter chapter 4 and verse 8…

1 Pet 4:8 *Above all, maintain constant LOVE for one another, for love covers a multitude of sins.* NRSV

One of the most difficult things to do is try to change for the good when everybody's speaking negatively about you and expecting nothing good from you;

And it's because love understands this is that it remains constant and gives every one ample *time* and *opportunity* to get back on their feet.

Once a person has come through *successfully*, love treats the person *like it never happened* (instead of, behaving like they owe them a debt from now on).

♥ *Love's Ability To Put Up With Anything*

One other aspect of *'bearing all things'* is brought out in 1st Corinthians chapter 9 and verse 12, where the apostle Paul writes…

1 Cor 9:12 *If you support others who preach to you, shouldn't we have an even greater right to be supported? Yet we have never used this right. We would rather put up with anything than put an obstacle in the way of the Good News about Christ.* NLT

The same Greek word we encountered in 1ˢᵗ Corinthians 13:7 that says 'love bears all things' is translated here as 'putting up with anything', which the apostle Paul is willing to do, so that nothing gets in the way of people receiving the Lord and getting saved.

As we conclude this quality, I'd like to *share a story* with you from MacArthur's commentary[90]; It says…

During Oliver Cromwell's reign as lord protector of England, a young soldier was sentenced to die.

The girl to whom he was engaged pleaded with Cromwell to spare the life of her beloved, but to no avail.

The young man was to be executed when the curfew bell sounded, but when the sexton repeatedly pulled the rope the bell made no sound.

The girl had climbed into the belfry and wrapped herself around the clappers so that it could not strike the bell.

Her body was smashed and bruised, but she did not let go until the clapper stopped swinging.

She managed to climb down, bruised and bleeding, to meet those awaiting the execution.

When she explained what she had done, Cromwell commuted the sentence.

A poet beautifully recorded the story as follows:

At his feet she told her story,
*   showed her hand all bruised and torn,*
And her sweet young face still haggard
*   with the anguish it had worn,*
Touched his heart with sudden pity,
*   lit his eyes with misty light.*
"Go, your lover lives," said Cromwell;
*   "Curfew will not ring tonight."*

---

90   John F. MacArthur, *The MacArthur New Testament Commentary*, *1 Corinthians*, copyright © 1984 by The Moody Bible Institute of Chicago, p.353

Chapter 14

LOVE BELIEVES ALL THINGS

❧ Love's Eagerness To Believe The Best

Returning to 1st Corinthians 13, we now come to the *fifth* of seven positive qualities that Paul says '*love is, and love does*', and that is, Love...

1 Cor 13:7b *...believes all things,...* NKJV

In other words, love is not *suspicious* or *distrusting*, but as Moffat says, it is always '*eager to believe the best*'; And if there's any doubt about a person's guilt or motivation, love will always look for the most favourable explanation.

Even when someone is accused of doing something wrong, love's first reaction is to consider them innocent, until *proven* guilty: It follows what the apostle Paul said in Philippians chapter 4 and verse 8, and that is...

Phil 4:8 *Finally, brothers, whatever is true, whatever is noble, whatever is right, whatever is pure, whatever is lovely, whatever is admirable--if anything is excellent or praiseworthy--think about such things.* NIV

In other words, love only thinks *'lovely thoughts'*, and makes a *firm* commitment to *retain* its *faith in people.*

And even if they are found to be guilty, love will always *credit them* with the *best motive* for their actions (looking for the *'why'* behind the *'what'*), because love *trusts*, has *confidence*, and *believes all things.*[91] (Hatred, on the other hand, thinks the worst.)

It's this quality of love that helps people *grow*, more than any other; the reason being, when people are thought well of, they tend to strive to *do* more, and *be* more than they are; The apostle Paul writes in 1ˢᵗ Corinthians chapter 10 and verse 24...

1 Cor 10:24 *Don't think only of your own good. Think of other Christians and what is best for them.* ᴺᴸᵀ

In fact, it is this quality of love that needs to be in operation in order for you to be *patient, kind,* and *forgiving* towards others, with the *right attitude.*

For example, it is almost *impossible* to be *patient* and *longsuffering* with someone if you're *not* willing to *believe* the *best* about them; Neither can you be truly *kind* towards them if you don't *see* the *best* in them.

♥ *It's The Thought That Counts*

Love that *'believes all things'* goes as far as actually *crediting* people with their *good intentions*, just as Paul did in 2ⁿᵈ Thessalonians chapter 1 and verse 11, which says...

2 Th 1:11 *And so we keep on praying for you, that our God will make you worthy of the life to which he called you. And we pray that God, by his power, will fulfil all your good intentions and faithful deeds.* ᴺᴸᵀ

---

91   John F. MacArthur, *The MacArthur New Testament Commentary, 1 Corinthians*, copyright © 1984 by The Moody Bible Institute of Chicago, p.354

That's amazing to me; That Paul didn't only pray for God to bless their *'faithful deeds'* but also their *'good intentions'* as well; Giving real meaning to the phrase, *"It's the thought that counts".*

❧ Love's Opposite – Believing The Worst

In direct opposition to all this is the incident recorded in Matthew chapter 12, where the Scribes and Pharisees *'believed the worst'* about Jesus, and constantly criticised Him for everything He did, and it says there, in verses 9 through 14...

Mat 12:9 And when He (Jesus) was departed thence, He went into their synagogue:

Mat 12:10 And, behold, there was a man which had his hand withered. And they asked Him, saying, Is it lawful to heal on the sabbath days? that they might accuse Him.

Mat 12:11 And He said unto them, What man shall there be among you, that shall have one sheep, and if it fall into a pit on the sabbath day, will he not lay hold on it, and lift it out?

Mat 12:12 How much then is a man better than a sheep? Wherefore it is lawful to do well on the sabbath days.

Mat 12:13 Then saith He to the man, Stretch forth thine hand. And he stretched it forth; and it was restored whole, like as the other.

Mat 12:14 Then the Pharisees went out, and held a council against Him, how they might destroy Him. KJV

What's interesting about all this is that, it wasn't God's laws He was breaking when he healed on the Sabbath Day, only their laws:

Laws that had been added by the Elders, and that were now in opposition to God's Own Laws.

In fact, their hatred for Him was so intense that, they didn't even acknowledge the miracle that had just taken place.

And when confronted, Jesus questions them, and shows them up for what they really are, *loveless* and *hypocritical* to which it says that they *'held council against Him'* in order to work out *'how they might destroy Him'*.

There will always be those that think that love is *'gullible'* because it chooses to *'…believe all things'*; However, remember that God's love is never without God's Holy Spirit and God's wisdom to lead, guide and direct it.

And, *just as a rule*, if there's ever *any question* about someone's guilt, it is *far* better to be wrong on the favourable side, than accuse someone of something they didn't do.

'Love is a harbour of trust' says MacArthur, and *'When that trust is broken, love's first reaction is to heal and restore.'*[92]

The apostle Paul says in Galatians chapter 6, verses 1 and 2…

Gal 6:1 *Brothers, if someone is caught in a sin, you who are spiritual should restore him gently. But watch yourself, or you also may be tempted.*

Gal 6:2 *Carry each other's burdens, and in this way you will fulfil the law of Christ.*[NIV]

---

92   John F. MacArthur, *The MacArthur New Testament Commentary, 1 Corinthians*, copyright © 1984 by The Moody Bible Institute of Chicago, p.354

Chapter 15

LOVE HOPES ALL THINGS

❧ Love's Hope

Turning once again to 1st Corinthians 13, we now come to the *sixth* of seven positive qualities that Paul says '*love is, and love does*', and that is, love…

1 Cor 13:7c …*hopes all things*… ᴺᴷᴶⱽ

This is by no means someone that is blind to reality and doesn't understand how satan operates in people's lives.

This is a person, that in spite of how 'hopeless' things may look in the natural, refuses to accept failure as final.

We see an excellent example of this, in what happened in Acts chapter 15, between Paul and Barnabas involving John Mark.

For those of you unfamiliar with this story, John Mark had some *confidence* and *commitment* issues on a previous missionary journey, which left Paul convinced that he was no good for the ministry while Barnabas believed that he deserved a second chance.

Let's pick up the story in Acts chapter 15 and verse 36, where it says…

Acts 15:36 Some time later Paul said to Barnabas, "Let us go back and visit the brothers in all the towns where we preached the word of the Lord and see how they are doing."

Acts 15:37 Barnabas wanted to take John, also called Mark, with them,

Acts 15:38 but Paul did not think it wise to take him, because he had deserted them in Pamphylia and had not continued with them in the work.

Acts 15:39 They had such a sharp disagreement that they parted company. Barnabas took Mark and sailed for Cyprus,

Acts 15:40 but Paul chose Silas and left, commended by the brothers to the grace of the Lord. NIV

Barnabas was a perfect example of *'love hopes all things'*, in the way that he stood up for John Mark, and chose to believe in him, and give him another chance, *hoping* for the *best* on their next missionary journey.

So profound was Mark's improvement that not only did Paul admit his mistake in 2nd Timothy 4:11 and say *"Get Mark and bring him with you, for he is useful in my ministry"*, but it is John Mark who ended up writing *the Gospel of Mark*.

Kistemaker[93] says *"Hope is patient, waiting for positive results that eventually may be realised."* He goes on to say, *"Hope is never focused on oneself but always on God, in Christ Jesus."*

MacArthur[94], in his commentary says, *"Even when belief in a loved one's goodness or repentance is shattered, love still hopes. When*

---

93   Simon J. Kistemaker, *1 Corinthians*, Baker Books, A Division of Baker Book House Co, Grand Rapids, Michigan 49516, July 2002 p.462

94   John F. MacArthur, *The MacArthur New Testament Commentary, 1 Corinthians*, copyright © 1984 by The Moody Bible Institute of Chicago, p.354

it runs out of faith, it holds on to hope. As long as God's grace is operative, human failure is never final."

Chapter 16

LOVE ENDURES ALL THINGS

❧ Love's Tenacity & Perseverance

We now come to the last quality mentioned in 1st Corinthians chapter 13 and verse 7, and that is, love…

1 Cor 13:7d … *endures all things.* NKJV

Kistemaker[95] says that the Greek word for 'endure' (Gk. 'hupo-meno':G5278) means *'to endure in times of pain, suffering, depri-vation, hatred, loss, and loneliness. …It implies perseverance and tenacity in all circumstances.'*

In other words, it takes great courage to walk in love that *endures*.

Only then can we be tenacious and persevere through all the at-tacks that the enemy brings against us, both *personally* and *circum-stantially*; And that includes suffering for the sake of the Gospel.

Peter knew what it meant to *'endure'* in love for what was right and godly, and wrote in 1st Peter chapter 2, verses 19 and 20…

95   Simon J. Kistemaker, *1 Corinthians*, Baker Books, A Division of Baker Book House Co, Grand Rapids, Michigan 49516, July 2002 p.462

1 Pet 2:19 For it is commendable if a man bears up under the pain of unjust suffering because he is conscious of God.

1 Pet 2:20 But how is it to your credit if you receive a beating for do-ing wrong and endure it? But if you suffer for doing good and you endure it, this is commendable before God.[NIV]

The apostle John had first hand experience with this and wrote in Revelation chapter 1 and verse 9…

Rev 1:9 I am John, your brother. In Jesus we are partners in suffering and in the Kingdom and in patient endurance. I was exiled to the island of Patmos for preaching the word of God and speaking about Jesus. (But God didn't leave him there, verse 10 says…)

Rev 1:10 It was the Lord's Day, and I was worshiping in the Spirit. Suddenly, I heard a loud voice behind me, a voice that sounded like a trumpet blast. (…and so began the Book of Revelation)[NLT mod.]

♥ *Never Failing Love*

In his commentary, *MacArthur*[96] says that the term *'endures all things'* is *'a military term used of an army's holding a vital position at all costs.*

Every hardship and every suffering was to be endured in order to hold fast.

Love holds fast to those it loves.

It endures all things at all costs.'

Stephen *displayed* this kind of *enduring love* when he was ridi-culed and stoned to death, in *Acts chapter 7*, and through it all said, in *verse 60,*"Lord, do not hold this sin against them."

Stephen did what Jesus had done with his crucifiers, in Luke

---

96   John F. MacArthur, *The MacArthur New Testament Commentary, 1 Corinthians*, copy-right © 1984 by The Moody Bible Institute of Chicago, p.355

chapter 23 and verse 34, and that is pray for them with an *enduring love…*

Luke 23:34b … *"Father, forgive them, for they do not know what they are doing."…* [NIV]

MacArthur[97] sums up the last four qualities of love that are brought out in verse 7, brilliantly, by saying…
Love bears, what otherwise is unbearable;
it believes, what otherwise is unbelievable;
It hopes, in what otherwise is hopeless;
and it endures, when anything less than love would give up.
After love bears, it believes.
After it believes, it hopes.
After it hopes, it endures.
There is no "after" for endurance, for endurance is the unending climax of love.
Now, we can *better* understand *why* the apostle Paul concluded in 1st Corinthians 13 and verse 8…

1 Cor 13:8a *Love never fails.* [NKJV]

When ever you hold your ground, and endure as the Spirit leads, it is *always rewarded.* Nothing you do for God *ever* goes *unnoticed.*
The apostle Paul was well aware of this and wrote in 2nd Timothy chapter 2 and verse 12…

2 Tim 2:12a *If we endure, We shall also reign with Him.* [NKJV]

And that's what *enduring love* has to look forward to for all eternity, *reigning* with our Lord and Saviour, Jesus Christ.

---

97   John F. MacArthur, *The MacArthur New Testament Commentary, 1 Corinthians*, copyright © 1984 by The Moody Bible Institute of Chicago, p.355

Chapter 17

THE BENEFITS &
MANIFESTATIONS OF LOVE

✣ A Look At Galatians 5:22-23

As we come to the close of this series, let's take a quick look at Galatians chapter 5, verses 22 and 23, which we touched on at the beginning of this study, which said...

Gal 5:22 But the fruit of the Spirit is love, joy, peace, patience, kindness, goodness, faithfulness,

Gal 5:23 gentleness and self-control. Against such things there is no law. NIV

Without going into a lot of detail, in the Greek, *'fruit'* is singular; That means that there is only *one fruit* of the spirit and it is love.[98]

As for the rest, they are all the expected *benefits* and the resulting *manifestations* of walking in the God-kind of love, that the

---

98 Bob Yandian, *'Galatians – The Spirit-Controlled Life'*. Copyright © 1985 by Bob Yandian. P.O. Box 35842, Tulsa, Oklahoma 74153. USA. p.236 (See also: L. Ann Jervis, *New International Biblical Commentary – Galatians* © 1999 by Hendrickson Publishers, Inc. P.O. Box 3473, Peabody, Massachusetts 01961-3473 p.150)

Galatian Christians so desperately needed to experience in their life.

Therefore, this list contains some of the exact same qualities of love that we saw in 1ˢᵗ Corinthians 13, such as:

Patience and *Kindness*, which were first qualities we looked at in detail;

Goodness – which is *generosity* of the heart – which we covered as a part of kindness;

Faithfulness – which speaks of *loyalty* which we covered in love *'believing'* and *'hoping all things'*;

Gentleness – which is the exact opposite of *'love is not angry'* (which we also covered) and;

Self-control – which we covered when looking at love *not being rude, selfish, proud, boastful,* and able to *endure all things.*

One difference between the Galatians list and the Corinthians list is that, the Corinthians list was more exhaustive and contained both positives and negatives, covering both *what love is* and *what love is not,* while the Galatians list was shorter with only *what love is.*

♥ *Love's Joy – Inner Strength*

The other *significant* difference, and what we'll be *majoring on* in this session, is the place of *joy* and *peace* in love, which we said earlier were classified as *'the benefits'* of *walking in love.*

In other words, the first benefit of walking in *love* is *joy,* followed closely by *peace;* Meaning the first thing you loose when you get out of love is *your joy* and *your peace.*

The Bible tells us in Nehemiah chapter 8 and verse 10…

Neh 8:10b …*for the joy of the LORD is your strength.* ᴷᴶⱽ

Yandian says, "This is not happiness, which is an outward expression of pleasure, a superficial emotion dependent upon our current

situation or circumstances. Joy is that deep-seated sense of well-being, which no outside circumstance can alter."⁹⁹

The way that God has *designed* for you to receive this *divine strength* is through time spent in prayer, fellowshipping with the Lord, and why Psalm 16 and verse 11 says...

Psa 16:11b ...*In Your presence is fullness of joy; At Your right hand are pleasures forevermore.* ᴺᴷᴶⱽ

Again, this is only possible while we're walking in love, which is what the apostle John again said in 1ˢᵗ John chapter 4 and verse 16, and that is...

1 John 4:16 *And we have known and believed the love that God has for us. God is love, and he who abides in love abides in God, and God in him.* ᴺᴷᴶⱽ

But not only do you have '*fullness of joy*' when you're *in Him* and *His presence*, but it is also the place where all your prayers are answered, which, in itself, according to John 16:24, leads back to '*fullness of joy*'; Jesus says there...

John 16:24 *Until now you have asked nothing in My name. Ask, and you will receive, that your joy may be full.* ᴺᴷᴶⱽ

Again, all this is only possible while you are walking in love and *Displaying Godly Character*.

♥ *Love's Peace – Inward Stability*
Now, added to joy, is also *peace*; Which also comes from God

99   Bob Yandian, *'Galatians – The Spirit-Controlled Life'*. Copyright © 1985 by Bob Yandian. P.O. Box 35842, Tulsa, Oklahoma 74153. USA. p.238

Who is Love, and which David brings out in Psalm 29 and verse 11, which says...

Psa 29:11 *The LORD will give strength to His people; The LORD will bless His people with peace.* NKJV

Yandian says, "*Peace is inward stability when everything about is falling apart. Like joy, it is a deep-seated assurance, a calm in the midst of the storms of life. The joy of the Lord allows us to sing at midnight while chained in prison with our feed in stocks. The peace of the Lord allows us to lied down and get a good night's sleep in the den of lions.*" [100]

Peace is of the *utmost importance* to us. It allows us to *hear God* and *be led by His Spirit*, which is why the apostle Peter writes in 1st Peter chapter 3 and verse 11...

1 Pet 3:11 *Let him turn away from evil and do good; Let him seek peace and pursue it.* NKJV

But again, this is only possible while we are *walking in love* and *staying away* from the things that Proverbs chapter 6, verses 17 through 19 says that God hates, and they are...

Prov 6:17 *A proud look, A lying tongue, Hands that shed innocent blood,*

Prov 6:18 *A heart that devises wicked plans, Feet that are swift in running to evil,*

Prov 6:19 *A false witness who speaks lies, And one who sows discord among brethren.* NKJV

God's *peace*, like *joy*, is *supernatural in nature*, and also comes

---

100 Bob Yandian, '*Galatians – The Spirit-Controlled Life*'. Copyright © 1985 by Bob Yandian. P.O. Box 35842, Tulsa, Oklahoma 74153. USA. p.239

from time spent in the presence of God, in prayer. That's why the apostle Paul said in Philippians chapter 4, verses 6 and 7…

Phil 4:6 *Be anxious for nothing, but in everything by prayer and supplication, with thanksgiving, let your requests be made known to God;*

Phil 4:7 *and the peace of God, which surpasses all understanding, will guard your hearts and minds through Christ Jesus.* NKJV

This *peace* has *nothing* to do with *reason:* This verse says that it '*surpasses all understanding*'.

In other words, this is the peace you get from God in the midst of a storm that allows you to stay calm and focused while everyone around you is falling apart.

It's a *peace* that you know you shouldn't have but is still there, regardless.

❧ Never Ending Light & Never Failing Love

Once again, all this is only available as we walk in *God's love* and *God's light, Displaying Godly Character,* and allowing God to do what only He can do, strengthen us and stabilise us supernaturally, to where *nothing* the devil does affects us any longer.

Furthermore, since *God is love* and *God is light, every time we walk in love and light* it will *always* bring *God* on the scene, and according to Jesus in Mark chapter 10 and verse 27…

Mark 10:27b *… with God all things are possible.* KJV

This is *the place of victory* that has *no end.*

It gives us greater insight and appreciation as to why the apostle Paul said, in 1ˢᵗ Corinthians chapter 13 and verse 8 that …

1 Cor 13:8a *Love never fails.* NKJV

MacArthur[101] says that the word *'fails'* in the Greek (Gk.*'ekpipto'*: G1601) has the basic meaning of *'falling'*, especially the idea of *'final falling'*, and was used of a flower or leaf that falls to the ground, withers and decays.

As for the word *'never'*, it refers to *time, not* to frequency, and the idea is that at no time will *divine love* ever *'fall, wither, or decay'*. By *nature* it is *permanent*.

Furthermore, *love cannot fail* because it shares *God's nature* and *God's eternity*.

Love *is* and *forever will be* the very *air* of heaven.

Throughout all eternity *love will never end*, just as *light will never cease*.

Success will not always be a part of love, but *love will always be a part of true spiritual success*.

So, when Paul says *'love never fails'*, he is not speaking of love's success or failures, but of its *lastingness* and its *permanence* as a *divine quality*: In short, he is saying that *'love outlasts any failures'*.

For Christians, *love is life*, just as *light is life*[102]; And *both are eternal*.

Love is the *supreme characteristic* of the *life* God gives because *love* is the supreme characteristic of God Himself. Again, that's 1st John 4:16, where the apostle John said…

1 John 4:16b *God is love, and he who abides in love abides in God, and God in him.* NKJV

And that's Paul's point. It is the truth he hoped the Corinthians would somehow *understand*, *accept* and *follow*.

---

101   John F. MacArthur, *The MacArthur New Testament Commentary, 1 Corinthians*, copyright © 1984 by The Moody Bible Institute of Chicago, p.358-359

102   **John 8:12** *Then Jesus spoke to them again, saying, "I am the light of the world. He who follows Me shall not walk in darkness, but have the light of life."* NKJV

He wanted them to be *successful in love: Successful in being like* God: Just like he would want it of *us* today.